CALL OF A COWARD

The God of Moses and
the Middle-Class Housewife

MARCIA MOSTON

THOMAS NELSON
Since 1798

NASHVILLE DALLAS MEXICO CITY RIO DE JANEIRO

Published in Nashville, Tennessee, by Thomas Nelson. Thomas Nelson is a registered trademark of Thomas Nelson, Inc.

Thomas Nelson, Inc., titles may be purchased in bulk for educational, business, fund-raising, or sales promotional use. For information, please e-mail SpecialMarkets@ThomasNelson.com.

Scripture quotations are taken from the NEW AMERICAN STANDARD BIBLE®, Copyright © The Lockman Foundation 1960, 1962, 1963, 1968, 1971, 1972, 1973, 1975, 1977, 1995. Used by permission.

ISBN: 978-1-4497-1996-8 (Westbow SC)
ISBN: 978-1-4497-1998-2 (Westbow HC)
ISBN: 978-1-4497-1997-5 (Westbow e-book)

Library of Congress Cataloging-in-Publication Data

Moston, Marcia.
    Call of a coward : following faith / Marcia Moston.
        p. cm.
    ISBN 978-0-8499-4730-8 (trade paper)
    1. Moston, Marcia. 2. Missionaries—New Jersey—Biography.
3. Missionaries—Guatemala—Biography. 4. Missions—Guatemala. I. Title.
    BV2843.G9M67 2012
    266.0092—dc23
    [B]
                                                                    2012000215

Printed in the United States of America

12 13 14 15 16 QG 6 5 4 3 2 1

To Bob

"For where you go, I will go, and where you lodge, I will lodge. Your people shall be my people, and your God, my God."

—Ruth 1:16

Contents

Acknowledgments

Once I began thinking about the people I wanted to acknowledge, I realized how many have played important roles in both the living of this story as well as in the telling. Truly "no man is an island," and I am grateful for all those who believed in me, prayed for me, and allowed me the space to make mistakes and continue on.

A special thanks to my former students at the Rutland Area Christian School, who traveled so many "elephant trails" with me; to Nancy Zins, who saw the teacher beyond the fledgling; to the people of the Brick Church, who gave of their hearts and homes; to my Monday night critique group for their support and insight; and to our many missionary friends whose selfless labors often go unseen. Thank you Scott, Natalie, Ben, Evan, and Philip for your love and goodwill in spite of the sacrifices along the journey. And thank you, Mom, for reading all those stories to me long before I could myself. Finally, thank you to the staff at Thomas Nelson, who helped to make the process painless.

This story spans more than a decade and intersects many lives. Although the veil of privacy is thin in these times of instant information, for various reasons I have changed several of the names throughout the book.

Part One

Coming

THE PROBLEM WITH PROMISING GOD YOU'LL FOL-LOW him wherever he leads is that you just might have to go. I suspect it would be easier if you were certain of his call-ing—like stepping out the door and seeing the lilac bush on fire and hearing a voice commanding you. But when it's your husband who is delivering the message—well, that leaves a little room for wonder.

At least that's how I felt when my husband rocked my comfortable, middle-class afternoon with his belief that God was calling us to pack up and move to a Mayan village in Guatemala.

1

Crossing Borders

"And the day came when the risk to remain tight in a bud was more painful than the risk it took to blossom."

—ANAïS NIN

I lowered the sheet from over my head. Slits of daylight squeezed through the gaps in the curtains and tumbled into the room. My eyes swept the walls, probing every corner. The eight-inch lizard that had disappeared behind the curtain the night before was nowhere in sight. Lily, our ten-year-old daughter, slept beside me, a mummified mound under the sheet. My husband, Bob, had tried to block her view as the long-tailed creature scooted across the wall just before we got into bed, but she had noted the look of alarm on his face and turned in time to see it.

I stared at the motel's whitewashed stucco ceiling spotted with brown bug splats. Today was Sunday, the day we would cross the border into Guatemala, the place we planned to live for the next year, the place we had been traveling thousands of miles from our home in New Jersey to reach.

We felt stronger now, more confident than we did three days ago when we had lingered in the dusty Texas border town of Brownsville and looked southward, reluctant to leave the security of the United States but determined to go. Trepidation gnawed at the edges of our courage as we considered how different that border crossing would be from the previous crossings over state lines. We went to the zoo, and then the bank, and made one more trip to the Laundromat. When we finally ran out of familiar things to do, we gathered our courage and drove across the Rio Grande.

To our immense relief, the actual crossing was relatively uneventful. Although there had been much discussion with our non-English-speaking clerk about how long our car was to be in the country and why there wasn't a watermark on our registration, in the end, we nodded, smiled, signed the forms, and went on our way.

People warned us about the dangers of driving through Mexico—the tire-eating potholes, the mountainous speed bumps that guarded the entrance to every little town, the banditos, and the perils of night driving. *Never*, but *never*, be on the roads after dark, they cautioned. Mexican drivers had some particularly disconcerting habits, such as driving with their headlights off and abandoning their cars in the road. Not to mention the stray animals and tipsy night revelers who traveled the centerline with equal abandon and unconcern about fast-moving vehicles.

More than a thousand miles stretched between us and language school—miles where we would have to buy gas and food and lodging. Neither of us spoke much Spanish. The fact that we were relying on my rudimentary vocabulary resurrected from high school lessons many years earlier wasn't very reassuring. I didn't have a good ear. When I had asked the person who answered the phone at the Guatemalan consulate in the States if he could speak English, he responded, "I am speaking English."

Although I could ask for directions, I couldn't understand the rapid, softly slurred responses and often misunderstood whether we had been told to go *derecho* (as in straight up to the volcano) or *derecha* (around the right side of it), a rather critical difference.

Bob, with his phrase book and handful of basic expressions, enthusiastically tried to communicate with everyone we encountered. He drew outright smiles from pan-faced gas attendants as he asked them in his thick Brooklyn accent, "*Llene mi tanque,*" but they nodded their understanding and filled the tank.

In one town, a policeman approached us as we pored over a map at the intersection, a confident smile on his face and a long gun hanging from his side. He rapped on Bob's window and said something that sounded more like a request than an offer of help. When we pretended not to understand, he tipped back his head and held his cupped hand to his mouth, indicating he wanted money for a drink. Condensing the whole thought that we were Christians and didn't want to pay bribes, Bob blurted out one of the few words he knew well, "Ah, no—*Jesucristo*." We blinked in amazement as the man threw up his hands in surrender at the mention of this name and retreated to the sidewalk.

Although in the past several days we had covered more than nine hundred miles of Mexican highway without mishap, we were edgy from being in a constant state of alertness. Our emotions raced back and forth between the excitement of adventure and the fear of unknown dangers.

Then, on the third day, unable to find a suitable motel, we were forced to continue late into the night. I kept my eyes glued straight ahead, watching for shadowy specters to rise out of the darkness. Except for an occasional "What's that?" no one spoke. Just when I thought my body could not possibly contain any more adrenaline, two red eyes pierced the blackness ahead of us.

It is doubtful that angels take the form of semitrailer trucks, but we welcomed it as one and hugged its taillights for miles, following it straight to the motel.

Bob stirred in the twin bed on the other side of the room. He searched the floor before pulling his feet from under the blankets and sat up. I smiled a little good-morning grin of victory. Wearing our triumphs over potholes and pesos and fear like souvenir pins on a hatband, we prepared for the final run to the Guatemalan border. I finished in the bathroom, stuffed my nightgown in my suitcase, and checked for six-legged creatures before closing it.

"Make sure you use the bathroom here," I advised Lily, well aware it might be the last clean one we would see in the next two hundred miles.

A few minutes later, Lily shrieked and bolted out the door. "There's a frog in the toilet!" We all peered over the bowl at the little sucker-toed green frog clinging to the sides of the toilet I had just flushed. I raised my eyes in a sigh of thanks that it had not decided to leap to safety while I was sitting there.

Closing the door of the room we shared with the lizard and the frog, we settled Lily in her nest among the trunks and bedding in the backseat. I folded the map to the southeastern part of Mexico as Bob turned onto the highway. We still had several hours of driving ahead of us through Chiapas, that turbulent Mexican state fraught with rebel activity and the consequent military roadblocks, before reaching the Guatemalan border.

It was a clear October morning. Mountain ranges rimmed the horizon. Lean, white cows stared dully from behind flimsy fences. Scrawny dogs ambled dangerously close to the edge of the highway, eliciting a few gasps from Lily. Chickens scurried aside, fluttered their wings, and settled back to pecking the hard dirt.

About the time the Pan American Highway bent its southerly course eastward, our animated chatter about life in the future replaced conversation about life in the States. We speculated about how we would communicate with the family we'd be living with while attending language school in Antigua, whether Lily would meet kids her age, and what our life would be like in the remote Mayan village where we intended to work with orphaned and widowed survivors of Guatemala's bloody civil war.

Unbeknownst to us, miles to the east at the same Guatemalan border we were heading for, young men with dark, slicked-back hair, older men wearing straw hats and baggy trousers, and poker-faced men in camouflage with big guns slung over their shoulders—the money changers, the translators, the guards, the vendors, and the hustlers—were gathering on this Sunday morning, as they did every other morning, waiting for opportunity to drive in from the west.

Signs warned us of the *frontera* ahead. We slowed for the approach to the border. Apprehension permeated the silence as we stared ahead at the throngs of people lining both sides of the road. The sight of our car, adorned with our Sears cargo carrier and trunks, energized the crowd. In animated unison, they moved toward us. Like long-awaited celebrities, we were swallowed up in the chattering mob. As we inched toward the barrier, brown arms clung to the car and banged on our windows. A cacophony of voices shouted out proffers of assistance.

"I help you get papers. I know what you do. Change money. It's Sunday, you no have problem; I help you. Speak English. Come with me. I show you."

I turned to Bob as he took a deep breath and prepared to enter the sea of grabbing hands. "If they make us open the car carrier and trunks, we might as well kiss everything good-bye. I'm afraid this mob will strip us clean," I said.

Bob opened the door, pointed to a guide, and disappeared in the throng. Lily and I sat inside the car, windows up, doors locked. Some of the more audacious boys sidled alongside the car. White-toothed, smiling faces peered at Lily. She stuffed her Walkman in her backpack and stared back at the bold, curious faces. We waited. My fear receded, regrouped into annoyance, then into boldness.

"Stay in the car," I ordered as I opened my door and faced the crowd. Looking straight into the faces of the ones closest to us, I silently dared them to touch our things—things we had so carefully chosen for our life in our adobe village. The crowd parted, settled back a few steps, and waited. Waiting for opportunity was their strength; defending my family was mine.

It was to be one of the first times, but by no means the last, that I took my stand and defied anyone to violate me or my family. Long minutes passed with no sign of Bob. I was getting worried but didn't dare leave the car to go find him. Finally he emerged, the chosen interpreter and an official stuck to his side. Once again, we and our car, properly stamped, inspected, and documented, were permitted to cross the imaginary line that defined the end of one world and the beginning of another.

As we passed beyond the crowd, I breathed a slow, deep sigh. It was a short-lived moment of relief. One of the tourist books I had read warned that just when you thought you were through, there was yet one more official who always asked for "two dollah."

We inched forward. He rose from his stool, his languid wave turning palm side up. He grinned and said, "Two dollah." Bob smiled and handed over two dollars. We would retake our stand against bribery another day.

Although it was late in the afternoon, we were determined to make it to Guatemala City where our contact, Raúl, lived.

"Why are all the cars turning off through that muddy field?" I asked as we kept on going straight ahead. Bob slammed on the brakes just short of an unobtrusive row of rocks. Lined up like miniature soldiers in silent formation, they blocked our passage. We had become quite familiar with most of the foreign road signs but were completely perplexed about this. We realized we had left the world of flashing barricades and orange cone markers but still expected something more official looking to mark a point of danger. Bob got out to investigate.

"There's no bridge," he said, getting back into the car. Apparently it had been blown out, a tactic we knew the leftist insurgents favored as a reminder that Guatemala's bloody, thirty-year-old civil war wasn't over. We backed up and took our place in the detour through the slippery mud-rutted field and crossed a low spot in the stream.

I tried to engage Lily in bright, brave mother-talk in order to stave off my anxiety, as it became increasingly clear we were once again going to be caught on the highway long after the sun had disappeared. At what we hoped was our last gas stop, I asked a man for directions. Trying to keep my eyes fixed on lips that hardly moved and arms that did, I gathered, from the last wave of his hand, that we were to turn right at the end of the street. That road, he said, would take us to the city. Carefully I repeated his instructions. He gave me a thin smile and a barely perceptible nod.

Invigorated by the prospect of the final lap, we headed down the street and turned the corner. Bob eyed the lonely stretch of rough road and came to a quick stop. "There's no way this road leads to a city."

Signaling to a man about to cross the street, we asked about the road. Both his English and his warning were clear. "No, no. Don't go that way. It goes to the volcano. It is very dangerous. Many bandits." He pointed to the way we were to go—completely opposite from the way the first man had directed. Thanking him and God for saving us from harm, we drove off into the night.

It was absolutely dark by the time we reached Guatemala City. Raúl wasn't answering his phone. We had no idea where to go. Horns blared, cars cut us off, and one-way signs directed us up one street and down another. We were exhausted. I saw a wedding party gathered in the doorway of a reception hall. The sight of their laughter, hugs, and intimacy, silhouetted against the warm hall light, drew me to seek their help. Bob double-parked the car. I jumped out and ran up to the group to ask directions. Although caught by surprise at the abrupt appearance of a distraught North American woman, they quickly understood the one coherent word I kept babbling— *hotel*—and all joined in offering suggestions and directions.

But it was too late. There wasn't one single synapse in my brain left firing. I understood nothing. Neurons stood at the edge and keeled over, unable to leap across the gap and make the connection. I thanked my kind advisors and got back into the car. Bob and Lily watched as my emotions came undone.

First, the intensity of being a stranger in a strange land seeped out, followed by the frustrations of spending seven days in a car. Then, like a suddenly freed logjam in a spring flood, all the fears, anxieties, and exhaustions of the past several months raced down the river and breached the dam. Everything washed away—the stoic wife, the brave mother, the obedient woman of God.

Bob noticed planes overhead and knew there had to be a hotel near an airport. By the time we checked in, with the exception of a few whimpering sounds, I managed to contain myself. The innkeeper, noting my distress, eyed Bob questioningly as he led us to our room.

Lily wrote her first letter to our home church: "We arrived in Guatemala. Mom cried a lot."

2

Wrestling What-Ifs

It's difficult to get your mind around trust.
You just have to do it.

We had come to Guatemala because we believed God was nudging us out of our well-meaning, comfortable lives to work at the home for widows and orphans that Bob had visited on a church mission trip the previous year. It had taken a lot of prodding on God's end and praying on ours to get to this point.

We were living in northwestern New Jersey at the time, not far from the Delaware River. On a pleasant but otherwise unremarkable summer afternoon while Bob was in Guatemala, I was busy laying a patio from some slate slabs I had discovered behind the garage of our hundred-year-old house. Quite unexpectedly, a singular thought pierced my Martha Stewart–homemaking moment.

Bob is going to come back and tell me he thinks we should move to Guatemala.

That's absurd, I countered to my unseen speaker. *Guatemala is a violent, dangerous place. Thousands of people have been killed in its civil war, and it's not even over. There are still pockets of guerrilla activity.* Dismissing the idea, I fitted another slab into position.

Bob came home two days later. "They need a couple to oversee the project" as the home for the widows and orphans was called. "Marsh, I believe God is calling us to Guatemala," he said.

Years earlier we had pledged to follow the Lord wherever he led, but after ten years of marriage, my fervor had settled around me like a cozy comforter on a winter's night. Zealous promises made on a beach under a starry sky lay buried under the security of paychecks and health insurance. Bob's return from his mission trip with the conviction that we go to Guatemala unleashed a torrent of fears that shattered my tidily defined world. Perhaps the Lord had tried to soften the impact by forewarning me, but my response was immediate.

"What? Are you crazy? Guatemala's dangerous. I don't even dare go there, to say nothing about taking our daughter. How can we possibly take Lily?" Besides, I challenged, how could we be sure it really was God who was calling us and not just a case of mission-trip afterglow?

I rationalized—we were already involved in Christian service. Bob was active in our church, and after work he attended Bible college before beginning the two-hour commute home from his job in the electrical union in NYC. I taught in our church's school. Certainly that was ministry enough.

I argued—the Peace Corps didn't even place people in the part of the country where the project was because of all the rebel activity. The area was such a hot spot there were still military checkpoints along the road.

And I worried—even if I mustered up enough faith for my own life, how could I knowingly put my daughter in the face of danger? Maybe real missionaries could do that, but I wouldn't dare. I led Brownie Scout troops and rescued stray cats.

Although more convinced of God's calling than I was, Bob, too, struggled about Lily. He tried to negotiate with God for her safety.

"Lord, if you assure me she will not be harmed, we'll go in a second," he promised.

God didn't negotiate.

Adamant as I was about not going, a glaring contradiction in my theology nagged me. I wondered how I could so easily believe in

Someone who created the universe, parted the Red Sea, and rose from the dead, but not trust him to take care of my daughter.

I thought I had settled the issue of trust, but this new situation forced me to examine my conviction. I believed God was real, present, and actively involved in my life, and that he wasn't just an idea stuck between the pages of my Bible or an impersonal force. Although I had to admit, my life hadn't needed any dramatically divine intervention of late. God had a lot of leeway to answer, or not, any prayers offered from my comfy couch. They weren't crisis-driven. But a road trip to a third-world country—now that required a highly engaged deity.

Like a toddler's trail of discarded toys, my past was already littered with cast-off gods that had failed to satisfy. As a child, I was as sure God existed as I was the church bell would clang on Sunday morning, but a college course in Eastern religions prompted me to set him aside and seek other forms of enlightenment.

I practiced transcendental meditation in hopes of raising my consciousness beyond my own self-awareness and of levitating my butt above my bed—both of which I failed to do. I chewed mind-altering mushrooms, searched the lines in my palms for direction, and calculated the planets' treks and times—all in pursuit of truth.

At one point, as far as I could see, there was only one option I hadn't explored: money. I was chasing down an opportunity to take up with a wealthy friend when my sister started praying for me. She was one of those enthusiastic Christians who left pamphlets on the backs of toilets and punctuated her sentences with "praise God." She annoyed me.

But one day, after my money man walked out the door and left me alone in a San Francisco apartment, four thousand miles from home, I turned to the God of my sister—Jesus—and made that mysterious crossing from unbelief to faith. The revelation and subsequent certainty of a God whose majesty and power were so great that he could create a universe so personal that he could know and care for me, redirected the course of my life. I wanted everything he had for me, and I wanted to give him everything I had.

So how was it that now, years later, supposedly older and wiser, I felt like a thumb-sucking, bed-wetting first grader?

Still hoping to give the Lord opportunity to withdraw the inspiration, I pretended to carry on life as it was before the Terribly Disrupting Thought. For several agonizing months, my fears contended with my faith, but images of an orphanage in the highlands of a faraway country played in the background of my mind, hunkered down in the recesses of my heart, and unsettled my previously peaceful life.

Finally, unable to get my mind around all the problems, practicalities, and possibilities, I came to the conclusion there were only two choices—either God was or he wasn't both supreme and personal. I was certain he was supreme, and the despair of imagining a life devoid of a personal God far surpassed any fear I had for our safety. And so, standing there in our kitchen with an obstinate conviction that this was what we were called to do, I surrendered to the fact that the One who revealed himself to Moses as I AM was substantially greater than all my "what-ifs."

I turned to Bob and agreed, "We need to go to Guatemala."

One of the persons involved with the home in Guatemala was actually visiting in the States at about the same time we made our decision to apply. He came to our house to discuss our role and responsibilities. Since the home was small and privately run, not accountable to any denomination or mission board, we wouldn't have to go through training or fulfill any special requirements.

The couple who had been overseeing it had left the previous

year, and except for a neighbor's intermittent involvement, no one was currently managing the place. But it wouldn't be as if we were on our own. This neighbor, José, often helped out and would be available to assist us when he was not away working out of the country. The women at the project cooked and tended to the children. We would be primarily responsible to oversee the money and general management.

Over a steak dinner it sounded simple enough. We would drive to Guatemala, rent a house in the village, and work with women and kids. I envisioned tutoring. Bob looked forward to discipling and sharing the gospel.

But the steps between here and there loomed large. I had no idea how to go from a middle-class home in New Jersey to one in a Mayan village. Relying on my modus operandi in previous times of bafflement, I simply did the next thing and listed our house in the "For Rent" section of the local paper. The couple who responded also agreed to take our cat. Lily declared *we* could go as missionaries, but *she* was going as a tourist. She didn't realize tourists didn't go where we were going.

Bob admitted it had taken the mission team over two hours to drive the twenty miles from the nearest paved road to the village where the project was located. We needed an SUV capable of maneuvering the four river crossings, steep climbs, and gutted roads. He stopped by a Range Rover dealer and watched a video of one submerged in water up to its windows. The thrill of adventure in a manly machine played all over his face as he told me about it.

Rather than being a source of comfort, the image of fording a river in a vehicle with fish at eye level terrified me. Besides, the price tag on the Range Rover was out of our reach. As much as I would have liked a Range Rover, I was relieved I wouldn't need a vehicle with a deep-water option. I researched the engine power in lower climbing gears and turning radiuses. A two-door Ford

Explorer caught our attention. We bought one off the lot at a reasonable price.

Having rented our house and settled the car issue, we reduced our seven rooms to bags, allotting ourselves one trunk each, plus one for household items. Bob shelved his union card. Lily gave her friends, Bethany and Aimee, split-heart, best-friends-forever necklaces. We hoisted the Sears cargo carrier atop the car, stuffed our trunks inside with enough room for Lily and a pillow, dropped off our saltwater fish at our friend's house, and turned south to Guatemala.

3

Lingering in Antigua

Even the dullest of minds, prompted by fear of a new situation or complacency in a familiar one, can produce the most convincing arguments to stop along the journey. But the Lord cuts to the heart of a matter. Ask, and he will put you back on track and direct your way.

The morning sun reflected brilliantly off the Toyota pickup trucks packed with brown-skinned men in white straw hats and women in vibrant fabrics. Horns blared as trucks, cars, and buses six lanes deep merged in two-lane streets. We were swept along, wide-eyed, gasping, and honking past Dunkin Donuts and Pizza Hut, fuming volcanoes, roadside *tiendas*, and clay-tiled haciendas.

In the light of a new day, the previous day's fears gave way to excitement. We followed the signs to Antigua, the town that, according to my research, was the place in Guatemala to attend language school. It had more than sixty schools to choose from and boasted an international flavor. The term *international* suggested to us a town acquainted with flushing toilets, hot water, and comfortable amenities. I thought it would be a good transition place for us, coming from our middle-class New Jersey home, before moving to our Mayan village.

Crude crosses and mounds of flowers lined the winding drop down the mountain pass into the old colonial city, itself sitting more than five thousand feet above sea level. I reminded Bob to slow down. I am not a good passenger, and all those death memorials, hairpin curves, and oblivious animals wandering on the roads were putting a prickly edge on our traveling relationship. Every time I thought we were about to go over the edge, I'd let out a yelp and startle Bob, who'd shout, "What? Don't do that!" In the next six months I would learn to live without a phone or refrigerator, and to buy beef straight off a hanging cow, but I never learned to stop gasping around the corkscrewed sheer drops.

Bob shifted into second gear as we leveled out onto a narrow, cobblestone street. Without an apparent intention of slowing down, a turquoise bus, crowned with as many people on top as inside, approached us at an unnervingly brisk pace.

We held our breath in fear and respect for that marvel of the Guatemalan highway: the chicken bus. These recycled North American school buses are as brightly painted as school girls on prom night. Emblazoned with names like *Esmeralda*, they lumber along, belching black smoke and honking relentlessly as they fearlessly pass poky pickup trucks on switchback curves. The passengers on top dangle their legs over the sides or wedge themselves in between baskets of chickens, boxes, and propane tanks as nonchalantly as if they were sitting in bleachers at a ball game. I was simultaneously intrigued with and terrified of the thought of riding one.

We continued along the narrow street to the center of town, each of us in silent assessment of the surroundings. It was dirty. Plastic baggies and used straws lay scattered. Paper flyers wafted in the breeze and settled down again in the gutter. The smell of urine drifted out from recessed corners. There were no modern buildings edging the skyline. Instead, ancient cathedral domes and squat bell towers, built in hopes of withstanding earthquakes, were silhouetted against the three colossal volcanoes—Agua, Acatenango, and Fuego—that loomed over the city in majestic and ominous silence. I later found out the cloud that constantly hovered over Fuego was not, as I had so comfortably surmised, an afternoon puff caught in the giant's gravity field, but rather a smoky warning of the roiling life within.

Everything was conflicted. Riotous tangles of orange and purple flowers spilled over high, dingy, whitewashed walls topped with shards of glass or loops of barbed wire. Young people in dreadlocks and backpacks mingled with indigenous women in woven skirts and braided hair. Open doorways spilled out onto sidewalks that heaved and tumbled, their reckless disarray left untouched from the last earthquake.

"Is this it?" Lily asked, her enthusiasm flattening.

In spite of having read about Antigua's colonial history and ancient ruins from several devastating earthquakes, in spite of knowing it was in a third-world country, in spite of knowing we were on a mission, not a vacation, we had still expected something more modern—more North American.

"I guess it is," Bob said, getting out and shutting the car door on our ethnocentric notions.

We stepped out into the central plaza, a confetti of colors and chaos, and sucked in the dry, dusty Guatemalan air that would now permeate every cell in our bodies and change the beating of our hearts.

"Señorita, which one you like? You like this one?" Two young boys carrying displays of woven bracelets zeroed in on Lily and followed her down the street, persistent in their offerings.

"I have good price for you. How much you pay?" one asked. At first, I was taken aback that they had approached a young girl and not her parents, but with entrepreneurial insight honed from an early age, they recognized the heart of a true shopper. And much to my surprise, they were right.

With a transformation as startling as Clark Kent's emergence from a phone booth sporting a Superman cape, Lily flung off her parental permission and foreign culture constraints, faced the boys head-on, and spoke her first Spanish sentence.

"*¿Cuánto cuesta?*"

With that simple question, "How much?" she stepped out of her mall-shop world and plunged into one of street barter. Although her Spanish vocabulary was limited, it was more than adequate for negotiating prices. She made her selection, haggled her final offer, and then, with a satisfied grin, tied her bracelet around her wrist. As though seeing the possibilities of Antigua in a whole new light, she eyed all the other vendors lining the sidewalk ahead of us.

I was much more intimidated by the idea of bartering, having learned very quickly there were unwritten rules, like not touching an item or asking its price unless you intended to buy it. This was particularly stressful if you didn't have the slightest idea how much something should cost. The casual response, "I'm just looking," didn't hold water with street vendors intent on finding your yielding point.

I didn't want to be the greedy, ugly North American, but I also didn't want to support a whole village, which is what I think happened with my first purchase, judging from the delight in the woman's eyes when I handed over the agreed-upon quetzales. I suspected she packed up for the day, filled her basket at the meat market, and went home to enjoy her good fortune.

We stopped to buy a soda and blinked as the storekeeper poured it out of the can into a plastic baggie, into which he plunked a straw. Declining to have our sneakers polished by the persistent shoe-shine boy who guaranteed he had the right colors, we made our way to our hotel, a seventeenth-century convent, where we would spend a few days until the school set us up with a family.

The Hotel Convento Santa Catalina is a survivor of the great earthquake of 1773 that destroyed many of the magnificent buildings of the city. The old convent is connected to a building on the other side of the street by a now-famous arch, which at one time allowed the nuns to cross over the street without being seen. Our room had an austere beauty that spoke of peace and lack of distraction. The rooms opened onto an interior courtyard with a fountain. As everywhere in the city, huge clay pots of geraniums and tropical foliage camouflaged crumbling walls and stained whitewash.

It was a lovely place for us to slow down and absorb the culture of this land to which we had come. Part of that adjustment involved getting used to noise. The ancient church bells didn't differentiate between praying nuns and sleeping tourists. Centuries later they still clanged away in regular intervals throughout the night. Finding it difficult to cuss at them within these sacrosanct walls, we'd either lie in bed and offer up a few prayers or try to ignore them and get back to sleep. This bell ringing was not, however, as unnerving as another popular custom we soon encountered in this land of festivals and celebrations.

Early one morning, a rapid series of loud cracks followed by a tremendous boom ripped through the predawn silence, startling us out of sleep. Bob bolted out of bed and ran to the window.

"What was that?" he yelled.

Heart thumping, I ran to see if Lily was all right. "The volcano must have blown, or maybe the guerrillas are attacking the city," I ventured. But the street was silent. There were no screaming sirens, no frantic people rushing out of doorways, no topless volcanoes spewing fiery innards into the sky. Perplexed and shaken, we returned to bed.

Our host later told us that this sleep-shattering, peace-rattling explosion was actually a very beloved custom. It was simply a family's way of letting their fifteen-year-old daughter know how special she was by announcing her birthday to the whole city with atmosphere-displacing firecrackers. This casual acceptance of incessantly tolling bells, early-morning firecrackers, nightlong parties broadcast over loudspeakers, and constantly crowing roosters in a land of gracious greetings and soft, round vowels never ceased to amaze me.

We enrolled in a six-week language program at the Christian Spanish Academy. The school connected us with a family from whom we rented two rooms, which were built on the roof of their house.

Our hostess, Elena, served our meals in her little kitchen and hovered over us, patiently trying to expand our vocabulary and understanding of the culture. Usually, this consisted of brief discussions about the food or directions to places of interest, but often Elena, encouraged by our apparent understanding, would launch into lengthier, more animated conversations, the content of which Bob and Lily relied upon me to interpret. Actually understanding about every fifth word, I often wondered if the story I relayed back to them at all resembled what she was telling us. One conversation was particularly troublesome. I imagined if I could hear it in simultaneous translation much as a UN delegate does, it might have sounded something like this:

Elena: "Do you know what your plans are? Will you still be living here at Christmas or moving to your village? I'd like to know so I can notify the school if the rooms are available to rent out again."

I translate to Bob and Lily: "She wants to know how long we are staying. She says we should stay on at school and not go to the village until after the holidays. I think she's inviting us to spend Christmas with her and her family."

I thought this a bit curious because we were not usually invited to family events, but I felt awkward questioning her. My forthright Yankee approach often stood out like a case of flatulence at a wedding. I didn't want to make her feel obligated to invite us if she hadn't, and so I responded as people so often do when they don't understand. I smiled, nodded my thanks, and gave the universal affirmative, "*Sí, gracias.*" As it turned out, we moved to our village before Christmas, thus thwarting any embarrassment caused by our unexpected arrival at the family festivities in our Christmas-morning pajamas.

We attended language school in the morning, then walked back home for the main meal of the day, after which we often enjoyed a siesta. All the banks and many of the stores and businesses closed for the two hours after the midday meal. At first I thought this was an inconvenient practice, but I quickly came to appreciate it. The effects of the heat, the high altitude, and the large midday meal all made for good cause to do as the locals and take a nap.

By the end of the second week, we shifted our identification from the tourists to the residents. One afternoon, as we were approaching our Explorer parked on the street, I heard some astonished tourists exclaim, "New Jersey!" when they saw the license plates. I had begun to forget how remarkable it was that we had driven here and that we lived here. Although constantly on the alert for pickpockets and ever wary of all the frighteningly young men wielding big guns on every corner and in front of every establishment, we were discovering Antigua's beauty and feeling more at home.

The grimy stucco walls that had so influenced our first impressions had now yielded their treasures. We discovered the flower-filled courtyards with fountains and cages of colorful, squawking parrots hidden behind the nondescript walls.

Each day we walked the mile to the Christian Spanish Academy, where we spent a few hours with our own tutors. Each day we sang out, *"Buenos días"* to the same vendors along the route. Each day we stopped at the same corner and chatted with the little girl who wore her basket of wares on her head as proudly as a queen holding court. And each day we mingled our footsteps deeper into Antigua's dust until we became so entrenched we began to reconsider our move to the rural village.

We had met several other North Americans at the language school and at an English-speaking church we sometimes attended. Many of the people who had come to Guatemala for some sort of mission remained in Antigua. There were plenty of opportunities to serve the poor, and its culturally rich base with pleasant housing and fellowship with other North Americans made a very persuasive argument to stay. The thought that we could "do good" right there in Antigua flitted across my mind and snuggled down next to the "This wouldn't be a bad place to live—far less intimidating than a remote mountain village" rationalization.

My resolve to continue with our impending move to the highlands was further weakened by an offer from a North American woman we met. She asked us to house-sit while she returned to the States. The prospect of staying on where I had become comfortable appealed to my sensibilities—we could learn more of the language and get more acclimated to the culture and—on I went, once again trying to persuade myself that I was being practical when I really knew I was procrastinating.

One restless night I got up to pray for direction. A picture of a village of clay-tile roofed houses hung on the wall in front me. I tried to ignore the visual as I opened my Bible and began reading. I'm sure the prophet Micah didn't have me in mind when he wrote his words three thousand years earlier, but that didn't stop God from using them to expose what I already knew in my heart—it was time to go to the village. The waves of double-mindedness ebbed away as I read:

> Now, why do you cry out loudly?
> Is there no king among you,
> Or has your counselor perished,
> That agony has gripped you like a woman in childbirth? . . .
> For now you will go out of the city,
> Dwell in the field . . .
> Arise and thresh, daughter of Zion. (Micah 4: 9, 10, 13)

As if on cue, the next day, Raúl, our contact, called to say he had arranged for us to visit the project the following week. I was finally going to see the place that had so rearranged my life.

4

No Turning Back

Those kicking and screaming death-throes moments when you realize you aren't and you can't are God's opportunities to show you he is and he can.

Raúl wants me to go on ahead with him to visit a sick pastor before we go up to the village. He's arranged for you and Lily to ride up with his friend Hernando, who is familiar with both the roads and the project. We will meet up with you there later." Bob anxiously searched my face for reaction. He was torn between concern for his family and Raúl's insistence on the importance of Bob accompanying him.

We were gathered in the living room of Hernando's house. It was the last stopping place before leaving towns and paved roads on the way up the mountain to the village. Raúl had just told us that not only was the electricity out in the village and we should buy candles, but he had expected us to bring our own bedding and hadn't made any sleeping arrangements. But not to worry, he said with the forte of a true missionary. He'd figure something out when we got there.

Now, he wanted to take Bob with him and leave Lily and me to ride up to the village with strangers whose language I could barely understand. I looked around the room. The women busied themselves in the open kitchen area. A cluster of men engaged in a lively discussion, accompanied by much hand waving, had gathered in the living area. Prompted by her mother, a girl I guessed to be a few years younger than Lily signaled her to go see the rabbit in the backyard. I tried valiantly to hold back both the fear and the fury that threatened to shatter the convivial family scene, an outburst that would be clearly understood in any language.

"I don't like it," I muttered. "I am afraid, and I hate going with people I don't know. And what about you? They say the banditos held up several people on the road this past weekend. You better get there before dark."

I shot a stormy glance at Raúl. Instead of being sympathetic to his act of service to the sick pastor, I felt hostile about his insensitivity to my fears of traveling to the village for the first time with strangers, rather than with my husband. I was beginning to suspect that my doubts about having the heart and stamina of a missionary were justified.

Hoping to convey some confidence and concern, Bob put his finger under my chin and lifted it up a notch. "You're a trooper. I love you."

Then he followed Raúl out the door.

I looked around. Lily and her new friend were communicating well. Apparently I was the only one who felt awkward. One of the women asked if I'd like to go to the market with her. We stopped and bought candles. Then I followed her into the open-stall meat section. Flies settled on the horns of rams' heads and buzzed around the tidy rows of pig snouts, hooves, and chicken feet. Unidentifiable body parts swung from rafters.

I watched anxiously as my hostess chose a piece of meat for our lunch. *No concerns about leaving out the Thanksgiving turkey here,* I thought. Saying grace before eating took on a whole new importance for me. A blithely spoken, "Lord, bless this food" came to mean a seriously earnest, "Kill it, purify it, and give me the grace to eat it."

After lunch, five of us piled into the old Isuzu. Hernando, the driver, knew some English, so between his bits of English and my fragmented Spanish, we were able to put together a whole conversation. I was wedged between Lily and Mita, a small Mayan woman who watched me and laughed heartily every time I gasped and clutched Lily as the outside tires skimmed the edge of the drop-off. Mita obviously had no idea that where I came from roads edging an abyss were supposed to have guardrails.

The road exceeded my worst expectations. Cliffs rose straight up on one side and plunged straight down on the other. The dusty, rutted trail between the two was wide enough for one vehicle. It was one thing to ride a scary road with a husband you could yell at; it was another to ride a scarier road with a stranger who said with the same equanimity, "There's a good view from the overlook up ahead," and "The brakes are bad; that's why I have to pump them."

Hernando downshifted, pumped the screeching brakes, and entered the river. I couldn't decide whether to look ahead at the slippery rocks on the steep bank, look behind to the place from where we had safely come, or simply bury my head in my lap. If I needed a sign from God, this was it. I decided there was no way I could ride this road to go shopping, to get our mail, to find a doctor, to do anything—ever. When, and if, I met up with Bob in the village, I was going to have to tell him so.

After two terrifying hours, we rounded a narrow pass. Hernando pointed in the distance and announced proudly, "There it is."

I lifted my gaze from the floorboards. My fears crumpled and folded at the sight of the panoramic majesty encircling us. Past the tall, close-in pines, past the glimpses of switchback, past the steep and deep valleys on whose sides adobe huts, with their terraced plots of stubby corn, clung tenaciously, the afternoon sun glittered off the tower of the old Spanish colonial church, which anchored the town center nestled at an altitude well over four thousand feet. A shadow of awe glided across my heart.

In retrospect, Hernando was the best possible person to show me the village for the first time. He loved the land, and it was through his love that I saw past the unlovely. Chickens protested as we shooed them from the path through the banana trees. Stray dogs trailed after Lily. Hernando pointed out the clumps of brazen bougainvillea that flaunted their purples and salmons and magentas over the adobe wall surrounding the property we would be renting. A coat of paint, Hernando said, and it would be nice, nodding to the water-stained walls of the adobe house.

The two rooms were arranged motel-style, opening directly into the yard. We had to go outside the main room and walk along the hard-packed dirt walkway, which was sheltered by a roofed overhang, to get to the bathroom or kitchen. The kitchen was absolutely bare except for the *pollo*—a cement firebox. Hernando told me that when the men came down from the hills to the market on Sundays, I would have to go out to the gate and whistle for one to bring his horse and unload its cargo of wood in my yard.

The sink, or *pila*, was a large cement reservoir about four feet square and four feet deep sitting in the middle of the yard. It had two basins on the front side that served as sinks for dishes and laundry. The *pila* was filled with the polluted water pumped from the river for a few hours each day. Plastic bowls and buckets served as scoops to draw the water from the basin well. Periodically, we would have to drain the whole thing, scrape the algae and water creatures from the sides, and douse it with a generous dose of Clorox.

A thin wire carried a weak but welcome current of electricity to a water heating unit, popularly known as a *widow-maker*, a moniker earned because it was attached directly to the shower pipe (which replaced the neutral) and delivered a strong zap if hit by a wet arm. There was a telegraph machine in the village, but no phone service. In spite of Hernando's assurances, my brain could form no picture as to how to operate from this home.

It was late in the day. Lily and I threw our backpacks on the floor and walked up the dusty road to the project. A row of kids, several barefoot, and three women wearing flip-flops solemnly examined our approach. I noticed some of the kids had bloodshot eyes, which I suspected was irritation from the dry dirt that swirled in the slightest breeze. The group was particularly intrigued with Lily, who was just as curious about them. Although there were other North Americans in the village, a *gringita*, or young North American girl, was uncommon. The kids gathered around her. Lily laughed, unconsciously flipping her purple retainer. Nine wide-eyed, curious kids peered into her mouth.

Eva Maria, the tallest and most outgoing, took charge of the welcome and sang "This Is the Day the Lord Has Made." Two girls, Julia and Blanca, dressed in their traditional village *traje*, followed us with shy smiles. They were actually three years older than Lily, but they were much smaller. Marco, a boy about thirteen, gave us a wide, toothy grin.

When Bob had visited on his previous mission trip, there were many more women and children. But now, for reasons unknown to us, only two families and a couple of men resided on the property. A partially completed brick building, originally intended as a church, now housed the carpentry shop, which was supposed to produce furniture to help sustain the project. The families slept in small rooms in a low-lying building across the rocky, cow pie–dotted yard.

The sun slid low in the sky. I kept looking anxiously for signs of a vehicle coming up the dusty road. Just as the sinking light slipped behind the mountain, Bob and Raúl arrived. We all gathered in the brick building for a service. The kids arranged benches in rows on the dirt floor. Little Pepe chased the cow away from the open doorway. Someone strung up a Coleman lantern. The younger kids sat close to their mothers, but the older ones, more curious than shy, moved in close to us.

A large, bright moon rose in the darkening sky. I looked down into Julia's deep, dark eyes and then shifted my gaze toward the open window. "It is the same moon I see back in New Jersey," I reflected. "But I feel as if I have been transported back in time thousands of years."

Raúl introduced Bob and offered to translate for him as he greeted the curious cluster of people who had stopped by for the impromptu church service. Built into Bob is an innate desire to make people feel comfortable, and these people would feel more comfortable, he surmised, if he spoke to them directly in Spanish. Although some of the women understood only the Quiché dialect, most of the people understood Spanish. The problem was Bob's Spanish. He launched forth in an emotional, heartfelt greeting, intending to express to them how much he loved to praise and serve God in his heart.

The kids giggled. Indigenous men stared with a confounded look on their faces. Raúl waited for Bob to finish and then said, "You made quite a first impression. You just told them you love to praise and serve God in women's underwear."

Someone rounded up three blankets and stained pieces of foam that were used as mattresses for visiting mission teams. We lugged them back to the house we would be renting when we moved up, spread them on the floor, and crawled under the blankets. Cleanliness was the least of my concerns. The sputtering remains of a candle cast imagined shadows of scorpions on the walls.

My fears about Lily were superseded by my own demons, which paraded before me. I commiserated with some of the heroes of faith in their weaker moments: Moses argued, Gideon fleeced, Jonah ran, and Peter sank. Then I remembered Jacob, who spent the night wrestling with an angel of the Lord, refusing to let go until he received a blessing. I needed the Lord to either release me from this commitment or give me the courage to rise above my fears.

"Lord, I've made a terrible mistake. I would like to work with those kids, and I long to know the women, but I am a coward. I cannot, I will not, ever drive that road again. It's far worse than I imagined. Do you hear me? I'm sorry. I just can't. It's too terrifying."

The specter of the empty kitchen superimposed itself over that of the road, unfurling new ribbons of tears down my face. "Besides, I have no idea how I am going to do the simplest of things here, like buy food or cook it. How can I take care of my family?" I wailed before succumbing to a fitful sleep.

Like raucous crows in a distant field, my worries awakened me. Bob and Lily seemed to have fared better with their sleep. I brushed my teeth in bottled water and splashed it on my puffy face. We gathered our backpacks and walked over to the neighbor's house for a breakfast of tortillas and beans. I felt miserable. Like a bride who realizes on her wedding day that she can't go through with her plan and has to face the expectant guests, I dreaded telling everyone we weren't coming. Bob and I hadn't had time to discuss the options, even if they included a return to New Jersey, but as far as I was concerned, once I drove down that road, I would never come back up. I hoped the Lord understood I was finished.

By the time we arrived at the project, the kids were waiting for us. One of the musicians from a visiting team led them in singing "I Have Decided to Follow Jesus (No Turning Back)"—in English, no less. Little Pepe teased Lily in an attempt to get her to chase him. Bob was involved in an animated discussion with the men—perhaps trying to reestablish his reputation after the previous night's faux pas.

The morning sun cast short shadows as it rose high above the four hills that stood guard over the village. Oralia, one of the mothers, approached me with a broad, strong-toothed smile. With directness uncharacteristic of this land of circular speech, she looked me in the eye and asked, "When are you coming to stay?"

I surveyed our ragtag crew. I suspected everyone had lice; no one had real shoes. No one seemed to care that the chickens hopped on the counters in the kitchen, or that the cows wandered through the broken fence into the yard, or that Maribel, the drippy-nosed toddler, lifted her skirt and squatted on the ground in front of a doorway. Everyone appeared to be content—happy even.

"In a few weeks," I replied.

5

Kingdom Business at the Motor Vehicle Department

God, the author of time, space, and order, seldom punches
our clocks or stays in our size-specified boxes. When he
wants to engage a heart, renew a mind, and save a soul,
anytime, anywhere, anyhow will do.

Having decided to proceed with the move to the village, we returned to Antigua to make the necessary preparations for an extended stay in the country.

Every time we ventured out by car, the transit police, who clustered on the side of the highway, spotted our white faces and orange New Jersey license plates. They hailed us over and subjected us to elaborate inspections of our papers, especially those for our car. Not wanting to give these men in blue any reason to add our SUV to their often vehicle-less force, we made sure everything was in order.

"I don't know how people who are in a country illegally can blend into the background of daily life." I said to Bob. "We have all the right papers, but we stick out like hookers at a Baptist convention."

Regardless of how legal we were, it was difficult not to get nervous by these shows of power. Stories abounded about people who had had their cars or licenses confiscated for drummed-up reasons. We had been told if we were in an accident with another vehicle, both drivers would go to jail for twenty-four hours until things were sorted out.

After a while, however, our apprehension turned to boldness. On one occasion, Lily suggested we test the literacy skills of the swaggering young cop who, having whistled us to the side of the road, approached Bob's window wearing that familiar smile of power.

"Give him the papers upside-down," Lil suggested, a mischievous glint reflecting from her eyes. Falling into cahoots with Lily, Bob rolled down his window and handed over the papers. The policeman walked toward the back of the car, put one foot up on the bumper, and studied the documents with the seriousness of a judge at a sentencing. Lily watched him from the corner of her eye. A big grin broke across her face.

"Don't you dare laugh," I warned. After several minutes, the young cop slowly righted his fistful of papers. Lily had the wisdom to look away, allowing him to save face and return them to us.

Eventually, when we saw the men in blue gathered on the road, we would either look the other way as we passed, or if they whistled and waved at us, we would smile, toot our horn, and innocently wave back as though they were good friends. This confused them. But if they were wearing khaki or drab-colored uniforms, it was another matter. We always stopped for the military.

However, as much as I appreciated a country's efforts to keep track of its visitors and their vehicles, I found the bureaucracy's love of minutia to be a major pain-in-the-neck, character-building opportunity. No one at *migración* spoke any of the words we learned in language school, nor did they speak (or at least admit to speaking) any English. Since I could read and write Spanish better than I could converse, I negotiated most of our business by notes passed through the slot under the window that protected the humorless clerk from my frustrations.

One clerk insisted we produce the original paper we received for our car at the border, even though we had a more recently authorized document. Our lament that it would mean a dangerous twelve-hour round-trip to retrieve it bounced off a face politely fixed in an imperturbable smile. Inwardly, I entertained a tirade of retorts: "Why are you making this so hard? Don't you know how much aid missionaries give this country? Do you know what would happen if all the North Americans who are helping just up and left?" Outwardly, I smiled. We were, after all, Christians here to help the cause of good and God.

We made the arduous trip to the village and back only to produce the necessary documents to a clerk who ignored them and stamped our original petition. My frustration was tempered by a thought about a mural I liked by artist E. H. Bashfield. It depicts pioneers moving westward. They walk along unaware of the angels hovering over them, bearing the symbols of technology and civilization that will follow. Perhaps we also had invisible heavenly beings escorting us, but all we could see was this meaningless time-and strength-sapping bureaucratic runaround.

That proved to be the case with Bob's driver's license. Messages along the North American grapevine apprised us of the necessity of acquiring a Guatemalan license. There were, however, as many stories as to how to do this as there were people who had attempted it. The most recent rumor was that Bob would have to take a blood test. We called the American embassy, which, in turn, called the jefe of transit police for us. Equipped with our up-to-date information from the chief amid all the flid legalities, we took our place in the license line.

The young man working the window ushered us into the office of the chief, who, because he had received a call from the embassy, assumed we were people of importance. Not knowing what to expect after we admitted we were working with a mission and didn't even know the name of the embassy person, we were relieved when he filled out our form and sent us on our way across town for verification of Bob's record. Much to our surprise, Jorge, our young clerk, simply walked away from his post at the window and offered to accompany us.

Lil and I followed behind, keeping Bob's and Jorge's bobbing heads in sight through the crowd. They were engaged in an animated conversation, which I thought remarkable because its intensity exceeded either one's fluency in the other's language. But if Bob were a body part, he'd be a mouth, and the one topic that flowed naturally from him was his love for Jesus. Thinking that not a likely topic at the moment, I wondered what he and the clerk could be so engrossed about. I should have known better.

Having secured the proper stamps and signatures certifying he wasn't a criminal, Bob emerged from the courthouse, Jorge by his side. For the second time that day, Jorge surprised us. He turned, clutched Bob's arm, and said, "I want to know this Jesus. Right here, right now." With that, he knelt down on the steps, indifferent to the passing crowds.

Being a more private person, I glanced about self-consciously. Where we came from, the sight of a person kneeling on the court-house steps would have attracted a bit of attention. But knowing there is no more glorious opportunity for a Christian than to par-ticipate in another person's encounter with the Lord, there, on the courthouse steps, on a sunny afternoon, en route to getting a driv-er's license, we all knelt to pray with our seeker clerk.

A few moments later, the happy man rose and led us back to the office, where Bob needed to get fingerprinted before the jefe signed off on the application, thus securing the Guatemalan license. It was already about three in the afternoon when we returned. Jorge handed Bob over to someone who whisked him away to the basement to get fingerprinted.

Lily and I were waiting on the main floor when two men carrying tanks with hoses burst through the door. They yelled something, which caused people to flee their offices. The window clerks shut down their posts. Everyone hurried outside. I had no idea what was happening. It looked like ghostbusters Bill Murray and Dan Aykroyd were about to purge the place. Someone rushed by me, turned, and explained—*cucarachas*.

The realization that they were about to attack government office cockroaches with what I feared was the equivalent of straight DDT snapped me to attention. "Wait; my husband is in the base-ment," I yelled. My entreaty fell on deaf ears. The men hoisted their nozzles and triggered a stream of cockroach-killing poison that emitted a cloudy mist through the room. Lily and I ran out to join the crowd in the courtyard. Five minutes later a fumigated Bob emerged triumphantly, displaying his inky fingers.

We were now minutes away from achieving the impossible. All we needed was the jefe's signature, but it was nearing closing time, and we were still clustered in the courtyard, waiting for the poisonous air to clear. I couldn't, I wouldn't, believe we had come so far only to be thwarted by cockroaches. The chief was standing with his men off to one side. The fumigators finished and signaled for us to return. Bob followed close on the chief's heels into his office.

The jefe signaled for his men to leave him alone with Bob. I waited anxiously outside. After a few minutes the door opened. Bob's grin preceded him. He held up a small square of paper. After we were outside, he told me the jefe said he was an honest man who was trying to clean up the corruption, but he feared for his life. To Bob's astonishment, he asked Bob to pray for him. Once again, on a sunny afternoon, en route to getting a driver's license, this time in a police chief's office, Bob prayed that God would save a life. Then, the jefe picked up his pen and signed his name on Bob's license.

Our friends Pat and Graci were duly impressed both with our prayer opportunities and Bob's license. Because they were fluent in Spanish, they helped many of the English-speaking missionaries maneuver the legal system, but they had never seen anyone obtain a license in one day.

Two weeks later we were ready for our move to the village. We spent the morning collecting the last of the stamps we needed for our visas. Bob suggested we have lunch at *Pollo Campero*, so we made the left turn into the driveway and parked the car. Before we could get out, a policeman appeared on Bob's side, smiled, greeted us (which I understood), and told us we had committed some offense (which I did not understand). He asked to see Bob's license—the miracle license we had obtained just weeks before. Bob passed it out the window. We watched in alarm as the man slowly rolled it between his fingers, and then, flashing us an unctuous smile, slid it into his shirt pocket.

I absolutely believe people are responsible for their own actions. I know self-control is a virtue, and I know not to argue with a policeman, especially one in a country in which I am the foreigner. But all this wisdom blurred as I saw the coveted license disappear in his blue shirt. All I remembered was the tidbit I had overheard friends relate a few weeks earlier: the traffic police weren't supposed to take your license.

I leaned around Bob and informed the looking-for-money cop, "You can't keep that." He ignored me and handed Bob a ticket. Finally understanding that we had turned on the wrong end of the divider, I acknowledged we would go right to the station and pay the fine, but that he had to give us back the license.

He smiled and said, "In a week or two."

Quickly forgetting that the God who had gotten us the document in the first place could just as easily protect it, I got out of the car, planted myself within a foot of the uniformed chest, and demanded, "What is your name and badge number?" I was so worked up, I couldn't understand the man's response, and so I kept yelling louder and louder, over and over, for him to give me his name and number.

To his credit and my good fortune, he never lost his composure. With a final, "We're going to the police station right now," I stomped back to the car. Smiling pleasantly as though we were discussing the beautiful day, the policeman handed Bob the license and calmly requested the ticket back. "*Buenos días,*" he said, and with a nod, disappeared as quickly as he had come.

Bob raised his eyebrows and looked at me without speaking. I suspected he was thanking God for the grace that had given him back his license and kept his wife out of jail.

6

Strangers

An act of kindness doesn't need an interpreter.

I peered out the rear window in hopes of catching a glimpse of the Toyota truck enveloped in the swirling cloud of thick orange dust trailing behind us. We weren't sure if the little pickup piled high with our belongings had managed the last river crossing.

Ann and Dan, an intrepid couple we had met at language school, had gamely offered to help us move to the village. Although they were from the Midwest, we discovered, small world that it is, that Dan had grown up in the same New Jersey town we were from. He was now in Guatemala working with a world organization that provided seed money to start small businesses in developing nations.

Both Ann and Dan loved the country's rugged beauty and were undaunted by our warnings that the drive was not for the faint of heart. They assured us they were confident in themselves and their truck. We hoped they still felt that way.

I caught sight of their own plume of dust as we hit the flats just before the village.

"Wow." A slightly pale-faced Ann stepped out of the truck. She gave me a concerned look as if to say, "Are you really going to live here?"

I understood her alarm, but had I already fought the battle between faith and fear, and I knew for certain this was where I wanted to be. We shifted our attention from the road to the house we were renting for fifty dollars a month.

Just as we finished unloading Dan's truck, the gate opened

and several men entered the yard. I knew they were relatives of the people who owned the house and thought they had come to help. But after nodding hello, they filed into the house and proceeded to remove all of the furniture and housewares from the two rooms we would be living in. Ann and I watched in silent disbelief as they stored everything in a third room, hung a padlock on the door, nodded good-bye, and left.

I suppose, being on *mañana* time, they just hadn't gotten to clearing out the furniture earlier and hadn't meant any offense. But as we stood there in the isolated starkness of strangers who had not yet crossed the line of trust and friendship that separated our hearts from theirs, I felt sad and unwelcomed. I wanted to tell them I had come to help the people of their land, not to steal their stuff. Not used to being the stranger, I was amazed to think we might be the ones viewed with suspicion. The reversal of perspective was not lost on my own conscience as I noted the lesson.

Thankful to discover they actually had left us a bed and a table, we made the bed for Dan and Ann, laid our new foam mattresses on the floor, cooked a pot of rice and beans, and collapsed into our beds.

The first morning in our new home dawned early. Ann, still wearing the rumpled, blue sweatshirt she had slept in, put coffee on the hot plate. We hadn't bought a refrigerator, so she mixed a jar of powdered milk. Lily stumbled out into the yard, where we had set up a picnic table under the overhang. In one hand she clutched a can of bug spray and in the other a hairbrush—the two items she had deemed necessary to face her first day.

After breakfast, our generous friends hugged us good-bye. Swallowing our own sense of loneliness, we fixed our faces in brave smiles and waved as they backed out the gate. Although they never returned to the village, they continued to be invaluable friends who would yet again be instrumental in helping us in time of need.

It was early December. We had arrived just in time to witness the village celebrate the burning of the devil. Throughout the day the incessant chanting and repetitive drumbeat drifted up the block from the Mayan temple. I peeked inside and saw a priest lighting candles in front of a canopied idol. Toward evening, the pungent smell of burning rubbish lingered in the air as people built fires in the street to purge their houses and lives from the evil of the past year. As with most celebrations in this country, the symbolism was graphically enacted.

Several of the children joined us in the street outside our gate. Bursts of firecrackers punctured the black night. We heard the approaching singing and watched as a shadowy figure swayed high on the shoulders of its bearers as they paraded it up the street. The "devil" was accompanied by a crowd of laughing, chanting, shouting, and drinking people.

The kids were curious but tense. I didn't know whether they were fearful for themselves or protective of us, but before the dark procession reached us, Julia tugged at my sleeve and whispered, "*Borrachos.*" Every procession had its escort of drunks, but ones weaving through the darkness with machetes in their hands were not to be reckoned with. They rated right up there alongside the devil. We hurried inside the yard and bolted the gate.

The first order of business on our home front was to put a barricade between us and the scorpions that dropped down from the open rafters. We gave one of the carpenters at the project money to buy wood for our ceilings. He took the money and a bus out of town.

After five days we gave up hope of his return. The kids felt bad for us and offered an explanation.

"He sniffs glue," they said.

When we had signed on back in New Jersey, we understood that we would be responsible for our own needs and that the basic support money for the home would be sent to us on a monthly basis. And so we were caught by surprise just before we moved up to the village when our contact handed us twenty dollars and told us that was all that was available at the moment, but that more would be sent up soon.

Between our own savings and gifts from friends, we had raised enough money to support ourselves, but we had not counted on personally supporting a home of widows and orphans. And we knew the women and kids would not understand that we didn't have money—we were, after all, North Americans, and they *all* had money.

Shortly after we arrived at the project, various storekeepers presented us with bills. Bob discovered that since no one had been overseeing the finances for many months, Mita and Oralia, the mothers at the project, had simply charged whatever they needed.

As the spokesperson for a Christian ministry, Bob believed he should establish a good name. He headed down the cobblestoned street to determine the damages. At each little store where he stopped, he encountered a dark-eyed, soft-spoken woman who smiled and wrote down a figure on a scrap of paper. After handing over the owed quetzales, Bob bid her good-bye, "*Vaya con Dios,*" and headed on to the next *tienda*.

It appeared that Oralia was more in charge than Mita, so we approached her and explained that we needed to pay for what we bought and wouldn't be running up tabs at the stores anymore. She and I worked on a budget. Variations of Monday's menu repeated through the week. Monday breakfast: beans with cheese; lunch: eggs with tomatoes; dinner: beans with rice. Although a budget was a new idea, Oralia grasped it immediately and agreed to buy food within our means. Our basic shopping list consisted of corn, beans, sugar, salt, oil, milk, coffee, and vegetables. When we could, we bought meat and fruit. But even when the funds were pinched, Oralia never complained about serving beans in three different ways on the same day if need be. The only thing I couldn't get Oralia to do was keep the chickens off the table.

One afternoon, Bob and Pedro, the one remaining carpenter, were in the middle of a discussion about what was to be done with the faltering carpentry project. Bob stopped midsentence and stared as two hunched-over figures, carrying what appeared to be logs on their backs, plodded steadily up the street straight toward the project. They marched inside the gate and dropped their loads on the ground at Bob's feet. Each log was sliced into boards, but left attached at the very bottom so it could be carried as a unit. The men looked expectantly at Bob.

"What do they want?" Bob asked.

"Money," Pedro said. "They say we ordered these boards for the carpentry shop, and now you owe them."

Bob looked at the two sweating men who had just lugged these logs on their backs down from the mountain. Each man was about four feet ten inches tall and of slight build. The return policy was clear—they weren't about to take the lumber back, even though we no longer needed it. Bob emptied his pockets of the expected amount and handed it to the men, who turned and marched away as solemnly as they had come.

Meanwhile, Pedro realized things were quickly changing and decided he had better get his own affairs in order. He claimed the project owed him money, which he wanted from the outstanding furniture sales. We had no way to verify this. Having grown up on the streets of Brooklyn, Bob recognized shtick when he heard it, but there were vast language and customs differences between life in Brooklyn and life in this Mayan village, and he wanted to give Pedro the benefit of the doubt. They eventually worked out an arrangement, and Pedro set up shop in town.

Meanwhile, we had an unexpected addition to our project family. One of the widows had a newborn baby. No one explained where she came from or acted as though anything was out of order. We soon realized things were more complicated than we had expected. It was becoming increasingly apparent we would need a lot sensitivity to surmount the language and culture barriers needed to get the kind of order we type A North American achiever believers envisioned.

Mita unwittingly was one of our clearest windows into this foreign world. One afternoon Bob approached her as she sat on the front step nursing her baby.

"How's the baby doing?" he asked, innocuously enough. Mita didn't speak much Spanish, but her answer was clear. Ignorant of an outside world, whose fascination with the female breast didn't include nursing a baby, she simply hoisted her blouse and cupped her hand under her full breast, indicating that although she had plenty of milk, the baby was not feeding. Her furrowed brow expressed her concern as she searched Bob's face for an answer. Bob hadn't expected this response to his casual question, but he quickly covered his surprise at both the sight of her bared breast and the expectation of his medical knowledge. He cast an unblinking glance at Mita.

"Yes, yes, I can see you have plenty of milk. I don't know why she isn't eating," he responded. "We'll have to get her to the clinic."

The baby did begin eating, and we later discovered Mita's assumption that North Americans knew about medicine was one commonly held by many of the villagers. People often came to our door or stopped us on the street in hopes we would have answers and cures for their pains and diseases. We prayed for miracles and dispensed lots of Tylenol.

Some days the strain of trying to see outside the borders of our North American middle-class work ethic was just too much. Frustrations, like grit caught in a gust of wind, eddied up and stung our vision and our own relationship. We quickly learned, however, "not to let the sun go down on our anger."

The nightly appearance of the scorpions seemed to be a metaphor for our own irritations. Inevitably, if we crawled into bed while harboring antagonism toward each other, the scorpions began their slow trek out from under our newly covered, straw-mat ceiling and down the walls. Sometimes they did this anyway, but always when we were angry.

They were an evil army with their pincer arms groping in front and their segmented tails arching over their bodies, ready to whip out and inject their neurotoxic weaponry. They marched slowly down the walls from the gaps in our mat ceilings. I always made Bob get them, which he easily did because, villainous as they looked, Bob was faster.

Nevertheless, these graphic portrayals of our own barbs and poisons were a powerful impetus for us to kiss and make up.

Although we had each other and our little family at the project, we were lonely for some other like-minded, English-speaking fellowship. Our thoughts went toward the North American couple we had replaced, who, we were told, now ran a nutrition center in another part of the village.

7

Friends

"Friendship, I fancy, means one heart between two."

—George Meredith

We were walking home for lunch after a productive morning at the project. Bob had finished stashing the corn in the new metal containers he bought to discourage the rats that had been ravaging the bags in the storage room. Oralia and I had finished the weekly shopping list.

The sputtering sound of a slow-moving vehicle approached us from behind. We stepped up to the curb as a sturdy three-wheeler with an attached wagon full of young children pulled alongside.

"Howdy," said a grinning, broad-shouldered, blond-haired man. "I'm Tim. Heard you were in town. Thought I'd give you some time to get settled before stopping by."

We hadn't been told much about Tim and his wife, Dena, but he certainly seemed friendly enough. I glanced over at the usual cluster of men who passed each afternoon under the shady eave of the corner house. Although they didn't understand a word we were saying, they watched us intently, as if they didn't know what to expect from this encounter of gringos.

"Why don't you come by later?" Tim said. "Dena would love to meet you. It's the house by the market, the one with the thirty-foot ham radio antenna towering over it." Off he went, bouncing over the uneven cobblestone street, kids hanging over the sides of the wagon.

We found their house on the busy corner in the middle of town. Tim met us at the door. I halted for a minute. Perhaps we had been told he was in a wheelchair, but I hadn't pinned the image on the robust, self-assured man we had just met with the wagonload of kids. Two dark-haired toddlers, obviously Mayan, chased each other around the table. One gave the other a push. "*Se cayó,*" he said with a grin. "He fell."

"Meet our sons, Caleb and Nathan," said Dena. She had a gracious, easy manner. I suspected she didn't get ruffled easily. The twins quickly latched onto Lily and led her off to see their toys. Dena pulled some cold sodas from the refrigerator. Unlike us, who still hadn't committed to the expense of a refrigerator, they were people who knew they were in for the long haul and had set up housekeeping accordingly. Passersby stood at the open windows and silently watched as we sat around the large table and swapped stories. I expected Dena to shoo them away, but she ignored them and kept her attention on us.

Sometimes it takes only a few minutes to realize your heart beats at the same rate as another's. That's the way it was with Tim and Dena and us. I suppose the chances of having things in common were pretty high considering we were all people who were willing to leave the security of the familiar and come to this particular place.

Dena had grown up on the mission field in Papua, New Guinea, and was comfortable with the idea of living in a foreign country. As a young married couple, she and Tim had trained in Haiti. When they heard of the need in Guatemala, they didn't hesitate to apply.

Although paralyzed from the chest down, Tim was willing to follow God wherever he led. But he hadn't always felt that way, he said. "When I was nineteen, I told God I was going to Colorado, and he could come along as my copilot. One day, a week after arriving in town, I decided to try out a friend's new motorcycle. Thirty seconds down the road, I leaned into a sharp curve, spun out, and corkscrewed headfirst into the dirt."

That brief moment forever altered the course of his life, but instead of becoming bitter, Tim became a man after God's heart. "God is my pilot now. I go along with him." he said with conviction. Tim believes all things are possible. He believes someday he will rise up out of that wheelchair. Meanwhile, he brings inspiration and hope to crippled and broken children in the homes he and Dena established in Guatemala and later in Costa Rica.

"Would you like to see our nutrition center? We can take a walk over; it's just down the block," Dena offered.

We stepped inside the enclosed compound. The center had quickly become known as a safe haven and place of healing for starving children. Sometimes children were dropped off but never returned for. Clean, well-organized rooms faced an open courtyard where children played. Dena introduced me to Tia Maria, a pleasant-faced woman who was hanging diapers on the line. Other aunties bustled in the kitchen or rocked babies. One little boy with a few scraggly wisps of hair growing on top of his bald head gave Dena a big smile. He wobbled over to her on skinny legs.

"He was so malnourished when he came a few weeks ago he didn't have any hair and couldn't walk. See how well he is doing," she said, giving him a proud hug.

As we headed back to their house, any reservations I had about this couple vanished. The high visibility of both their home and their ministry had also helped dispel many of the suspicions that the villagers held toward foreigners.

"One day, two years ago," Dena said, "Tim was at the ministry, and I was home alone. A small Mayan man, accompanied by a female translator, came to my door. She told me the man's wife had died in childbirth. She'd had twins, but he had no way to care for them. He wanted to know if we would take them."

Dena knew if she didn't give him a direct answer right then, he would leave and not come back. But acquiring two children while her husband was away wasn't a good marriage move.

That night, after Tim returned and they had a chance to talk, Dena got the village nurse to take her on his four-wheeler out to the tiny mountain community where the father lived. They entered the dark hut lit only by a smoldering oiled rag. An old woman, who Dena was told was the grandmother, studied Dena, her eyes dark and unreadable. She pointed to a little bundle in the corner. Dena pulled back the piece of cloth covering the two tiny boys. She examined the perfectly formed tiny fingers and toes. (When she later weighed them, one weighed four pounds, the other two.)

Concerned that the family might want her to raise the children and then want them back at a future time, Dena clarified what it would mean if she took them. Using the nurse to translate her response into the family's native dialect, Dena said they needed to understand that if she took the boys, they would be hers forever, and that although they had property in the village, they might not always live there. She told the father she would come back in two days for his answer.

Two days later Dena waited anxiously outside the hut for the father to return from the field. Several hours later he appeared, leading his mule laden with firewood. Seeing her, he simply nodded, and with that simple gesture, agreed to the greatest sacrifice a father could give.

"And look at them now," Dena said.

I followed her eyes down the street as the compact unit moved slowly over the rough cobblestone. Like a set of parentheses defining a matter of importance, two little boys in red shorts, one on each side, clung to Tim's wheelchair as they headed home.

Tim and Dena became invaluable friends and sources of support. They were people who were comfortable with themselves, their

God, and their place in the culture in which they lived. Tim was a visionary who always had a project in the works. When Bob told him about our unexpected lumber delivery, Tim immediately offered to buy it.

Every Sunday he invited us over to make phone patches to our family and friends in the States. One of his ham radio contacts generously absorbed the long-distance phone charges and patched the connection through to whatever number we gave them. I hadn't realized how much I missed hearing the voices of my family and friends. Even though there was a reception delay between sentences and we had to remember to say "over" when we were through, we hung on to every word, relishing the warmth of contact delivered over invisible waves.

Dena became my mentor both in mission matters and survival ones. It was because of her we got to eat beef once.

"Every Saturday the butcher kills a cow. I'll take you to his shop," she offered. The following Saturday, we stood in the open doorway of the one-room butcher shop. A hideless cow hung from the rafters.

"You tell him which part you want, and he'll chop it off," she said, indicating the bloody hatchet stuck in a block of wood. I hardly knew what part of an animal the chunks of meat neatly packaged in Styrofoam trays came from, and I certainly had no idea what part of this animal I'd want to eat. Dena ordered a couple of pounds and pointed to a section of the suspended carcass. With a deft stroke, the butcher whacked off a chunk and held it up for our inspection.

"Is that good?" Dena asked.

I felt as though I'd swallowed a frog but configured my face as if to say, "Yeah, it's great. Just like I always buy it."

Mentally, I moved beans to the top of my protein-source list.

8

What's a Woman to Do with All Her Time?

When cultures collide, a shared laugh makes a strong bridge.

Not to be outdone by a few predawn roosters, the chicken bus heralded each new day at 4:00 a.m. It wended its way through the side streets, exuberantly announcing its departure with unapologetic honking. No one could blame the bus if he overslept in this clockless village. I loved the early morning hours and often wrapped up in a shawl and slipped out to the patio to absorb the sounds and smells of a village awaking.

Shortly after the horn of the bus faded down the road, the roosters joined in, followed by the roar of the *molina*, the mill, as it fired up in anticipation of the daily parade of women who arrived with baskets of corn on their heads and left with ground meal for the day's tortillas.

These strong, hardworking women, dressed in their colorful village wraps and elegantly plaited headdresses—statuesque princesses in plastic flip-flops—emerged from their dirt-floor adobe houses, seldom stumbling on the dirt paths or cobblestone streets although laden with babies on their backs, and baskets of tortillas or bundles of wood on their heads. There seemed to be no limit as to what they could carry on their bodies. I once watched a woman glide along the rock-strewn road with a propane tank balanced on top of her coiled braid and a bouquet of white calla lilies in her arm.

They had a fortitude and strength for survival. Although I couldn't carry a basket on my head or baby in a blanket on my back, I suspected a woman's heart beat the same no matter where in the world she walked, and I was restless to get beyond the veil of the foreigner.

About the time the first shafts of pink light cleared the hills, the night air gave way to wafts of wood smoke as the women began their day. By 6:00 a.m. the melody of hands patting cornmeal into tortillas drifted through the backyards. Often, around 7:00 a.m. Eva Maria showed up at the gate and called in her high-pitched voice, "*Hermana* Marcia, are you having *panqueques* for breakfast?" Even if I wasn't ready to start my day with company, I could never resist her hopeful smile. Eva Maria wanted to go to the United States someday. I had no doubt that her optimistic tenacity would get her there.

I sat at our outdoor table, protected by a roofed overhang, and gazed out at the hills in the distance. The four hills cornering the village were topped with altars to the Mayan spirits. One day before we realized this, we had decided to hike to the top of one. I chickened out halfway because the steep, grassy slope was dry and slippery, and there was nothing to hang on to, but Bob and Lily climbed to the top. There they found mounds of stone covered with candle wax. Identifying with the impulsive Peter in spirit, Bob's first impulse was to dismantle the altar and defy the false gods, but wisdom had her way. Instead, he uttered a proclamation in the name of Jesus and decided to wait on the Lord before launching into a deep-seated battle.

As I snuggled in my shawl on the patio, the sun emerged in its daily splendor. I thought about the differences in implications of beliefs. You could be held in bondage, fear, and superstition because you believed a capricious god controlled the earth, wind, and fire; or you could be free, secure, and confident in the knowledge that your God not only created laws of order but gave you the authority over his creation. When we moved to the village, I had wanted to be careful about confusing culture with Christianity, but the more I observed, the more I understood the good of God's ways in the everyday functions of life.

I tried to explain the importance of this to Lily one day as we watched some men do hours of heavy labor without the use of anything more than some buckets and shovels, not even a wheelbarrow. In the politically incorrect innocence of a ten-year-old, Lily asked, "Why are these people so backward? Are they born that way?"

I knew that, rather than being fresh, she was genuinely befuddled by the lack of industry and technological development that characterized much of the country. For the first time, I understood how much a people's worldview affects their lives, even their socioeconomic development. Seizing a teachable moment, I told Lily about the many scientific discoveries that originated from a belief in an orderly world, such as Matthew Maury's discovery of the currents after reading about the "paths in the sea" from the book of Psalms.

My morning reveries were usually interrupted by the sound of the water gushing in the pipes. It was important to fill the *pila* because the polluted water pumped from the river was available for only a few hours each day.

I rose and made coffee, boiling it on the two-burner electric tabletop stove we used for quick cooking in place of the wood-stove. After breakfast, I swept the yard around our walkways. During the day, the surface dirt dried and crumbled. It clung to our shoes and sifted into the house, settling over everything. But the hard-packed soil underneath was solid as a New York sidewalk, for a few hours, anyway.

"If only my friends could see me," I mused, "sweeping a dirt yard."

Our village was the hub for the sixty or so tiny communities tucked in the mountainsides. Sunday may be the revered Sabbath day in many parts of the world, but here it was market day. Since we had arrived in town on a Friday, I had no idea what to expect on my first day grocery shopping.

Bob, Lily, and I joined the streams of colorfully dressed people funneling into the town square. We looked at them, and they looked at us. Obviously we were the newcomers in this mountain hideaway. Women tugged reluctant pigs attached to thin ropes. Others carried baskets crammed with young, spiky-haired roosters.

We greeted the barber, who had set up a chair and mirror on the curb and offered to shave and shear whosoever didn't mind the community comb. Bob and Lily posed for a photo. Just as I snapped the picture, a shrill shriek diverted my attention. A baby sitting on the side of the street, outstretched arm pointing toward Bob, screamed as if he'd just seen the boogeyman.

Vendors piled their plastic wares on rickety tables; others dumped their corn, tomatoes, and potatoes on blue tarps spread out on the rubbish-riddled street. Nervously, I rehearsed how I would make my first purchase. I walked past the tomatoes spilling onto the dirty street and searched for a vendor who had purchased a table for his wares. This was a painfully long way from my local supermarket.

Finally mustering up enough courage to buy some potatoes, I asked, "*¿Cuántas?*"

The craggy-faced man eyed me and placed a few spotted potatoes on a scale I suspected had long ago lost its measure of fair weight. I simply nodded my agreement with his price.

Villages were known for their products; some specialized in woven items, others pottery. Our village was known for its straw mats. On market day, tall rolls of woven mats leaned against buildings on every corner. We bought lots of mats. We stapled them to our rafters. We put them on our cement floors. We spread them over our dirt walkways.

Although I planned to stock up on boxed and canned goods on our monthly expeditions to Guatemala City, I bought our fruits and vegetables at the local weekly market. Initially I had qualms about buying my vegetables off the street, but necessity is a great neutralizer of finickiness. So is Clorox. I'd spend the hour after I got back from the market soaking all my fruits and vegetables in a bleach solution and then rinsing them in boiled water. The daily chores—sweeping the yard, washing clothes by hand, and boiling water to do the dishes and wash the vegetables—took so much time and energy.

I had debated whether to hire a wash woman. On the one hand, most anyone would work cheaper than I thought reasonable. On the other, there was an understood community wage that if transgressed would upset the economic equilibrium. Actually, there were two pay rates—one for the locals and one for the gringos. Undecided, I scrubbed my own clothes by hand until I got a flesh-eating infection in my finger that required my keeping it out of water. The woman I hired was such a wizard with her soap bar, I would have traded in my washing machine for her. She actually scrubbed an oil stain out of Bob's pants. Between the strong soap and the beating sun, our clothes got pretty threadbare, but they were clean.

Glad to be relieved of a chore that took so many hours of my time, I spent more time at the project, where I discovered Mita and Oralia could hardly imagine what any woman would do with herself if she weren't occupied with these time-consuming tasks.

Oralia, the strong, enterprising mother of several of the children at the project, had a husband in another village. Many of the women stayed with their abusive or negligent husbands, but Oralia had taken her five children and moved to the project. By the time we arrived, Oralia's husband had reportedly become a Christian and wanted his family back. Oralia was willing, so Bob, with the interpretive help of José, began working with them on reconciliation. Meanwhile, Oralia continued on at the project with us until all agreed it was safe to move back to her husband's village.

Oralia spoke both Spanish and Quiché and translated for Mita, who spoke little Spanish. She liked interacting with the North Americans and had no qualms about dressing her kids in clothes typical of any North American child. Her children wore the skirts, pants, and T-shirts that arrived in the mission boxes. Eva Maria appeared in our doorway one afternoon proudly sporting heart-shaped sunglasses, a cartoon character T-shirt, and a flounced skirt. She asked me to take her picture.

On the other hand, Julia and Blanca, Mita's daughters, clung, as did their mother, to their ancient roots. One day Lily dressed them in some of her clothes. Like poster children for police mug shots, they posed long enough for Lily to get their picture and then ditched their rugby shirts, jeans, and T-shirts for the red-and-orange-striped *cortes* and lace trimmed *huipiles*, the woven skirts and colorful blouses, that identified the village.

Mita had lost her husband during the country's civil war. When I asked her what had happened, she sliced her finger across her neck and nodded her head, her sad eyes telling me volumes about the way life was for a people caught in the crosshairs of a government and an insurrection.

One afternoon Oralia invited me into her room. She cleared a pile of blankets so Mita and I could sit on the two hard beds. Dust motes floated in the sunshine streaming through the glassless window. Like schoolgirls sharing afternoon secrets, they plied me with questions.

"What is your home like in the United States?" Oralia asked.

Mita waited expectantly. I looked out the doorway a
young daughter swept the dirt. "Well, I have a mac
washes our clothes, and one that washes our dishes, an
sucks up the dirt from the floor," I said. Oralia translated
whose dark eyes widened. Mita said something in her di
they both laughed.

"What?" I asked.

"Mita thinks since you have so little to do, you must l
with Roberto all day."

I didn't even attempt to explain myself. I just relishe
of sharing a joke with these women in this crowded li
with boxes of clothing stacked in the corner and chickens
at the door.

9

A Cancer Researcher and a
Mayan Named Marco

Never underestimate God.

There are times when God's presence seems as hidden as a flock of grackles in a leafy tree. You don't even know they are there until, in a sudden, startling flash, thousands of beating wings burst into flight.

It was the week before Christmas. We stuck a large pine branch in a jar and hung a few decorations on it that Pat and Graci, our friends from Antigua who specialized in supporting field missionaries, had brought up on a surprise visit. I had bought some miniature clay animals beforehand for Lily and had candy and trinkets for the kids. Nevertheless, we knew they had had enough experience with gift-bearing North American mission teams to hope for more substantial presents. We did not want to disappoint them, but we had just enough money to buy food. I knew my God was faithful, but considering we had no phone or reliable mail service in this town, I thought he was running a bit short of time.

The afternoon bus boasted its arrival and stopped at the corner. A few minutes later our gate swung open and in walked Jason, a young man we had befriended at language school, with another man whom Jason introduced as his friend John. John was a cancer researcher from Chicago on vacation in Guatemala. With the adventurous spirit of youth on their side, they had decided it would be great fun to take the chicken bus on the eight-hour ride to our village even though, in those days before cell phones, they had no way of knowing whether we would be there.

We were delighted to have our second set of visitors in a month, but since I still didn't have a refrigerator, I didn't have much to offer them.

"Let's have chicken," Jason suggested. Visions of Saran-wrapped chicken breasts floated past my mind. The nearest supermarket was hours away.

"We'll have to ask around," I said. "Maybe someone has one for sale."

Bob, Lily, Jason, John, and I headed down the street in search of a chicken. The first señora we met was more than willing to help. I silenced my gasp as she, with the unflappable efficiency of motherhood, used her bare hand to swipe a runny glob from the nose of a dirty-faced boy clinging to her apron.

"I think the woman down the street has one," she suggested. "I will go with you to ask." Now we were a procession of seven marching down the dusty cobblestone street. Five gringos and two Latinos constituted an interesting happening in this sleepy village, and soon a few more kids joined our procession.

That señora did not, in fact, have any chickens for sale, but she was certain the old lady who lived up the lane did. We all filed up the street to the old lady's brown, water-stained adobe hut. She nodded enthusiastically when our señora guide explained what we wanted. The toothless woman grinned and pointed out a scrawny rooster, who eyed us suspiciously. That I continue to eat chicken to this day does not speak well of my sensitivity. We all formed a circle around the hapless rooster as the old lady chased it.

Cornering it, she grabbed it by its scrawny neck and offered him up to whoever was the appointed grim reaper. We all looked at Jason.

"I'll help you," Lily offered. I think she was so happy to see a North American visitor within ten years of her own age she would have wrung the rooster's neck herself. Lily and Jason went behind the house to prepare the rooster for dinner. We paid the old lady for her provisions and went home. I cooked the carcass on my woodstove, but it was so tough I don't think even the manners of guests could pretend otherwise.

The kids at the project were thrilled to have visitors. Five-year-old Carmen captured Jason's heart and managed to win the baseball cap right off his head. John, the man who spent his life peering through microscopes, immersed himself in the daily routines of the children. For a man familiar with the microcosm of deadly bacteria and viruses, he didn't flinch a bit when grubby children hugged his face and clambered over him. We were all sad to see them go. But just before they caught the bus back to Antigua, John presented us with an envelope.

"I told my friends that instead of giving Christmas presents, I was going to give a gift to the kids in Guatemala in their names."

After we hugged and said our good-byes, we opened his envelope. I thumbed through the roll of twenty-dollar bills. There was enough Christmas money to buy all the children shoes, a small toy, and school supplies.

I like God's style. He could have sent some money through the usual channels, and it would have been welcome enough, but with divine flourish, he took a cancer researcher from thousands of miles away and put him on a chicken bus to our remote village, just so he could deliver a blessing.

Oh, me of little faith. Why had I doubted that just because it was the week before Christmas, and we had no money or presents, he would come through?

Probably for the same reason I kept worrying about Lily. At

times my faith had the attention span of a four-year-old. I had to keep wrestling down the conviction that God was more in control of her life than I was. She was our baby and only girl, and somehow it seemed that during the fourteen years between her and my first child, the world had become a scarier place to raise children. Maybe I had just become more responsible, or maybe I had begun to set my trust on a more secure lifestyle.

I raised my son in the aftermath of my discovery of the freedoms of the '60s. I lugged him across country in my blue Volkswagen Bug, cloth diapers flapping out the window to dry, spent a summer with him in a tepee on a Vermont mountaintop, and taught him to shoot tin cans from the front porch of our country cabin. The most constant things in his life were his yellow, quilted sleeping bag and case of Matchbox cars.

By the time Lily came along, I was living a secure life under God and my husband.

But now we resided in a village where nothing was familiar: a village where men drove herds of cows instead of cars down the main street at the end of a day, a village where pagan gods vied with saints and Mary and Jesus in rowdy processions, a village where machismo and cheap drink made dangerous bedfellows.

Girls were considered women at a young age here. Although she was only ten, Lily was tall. Several of the young men and boys who spent their afternoons sitting on the street curb clicked their tongues and whistled when she walked by. One, on the other hand, disliked her and pelted her with stones (which she later told me she threw back). Bob had delivered a very clear she's-my-daughter, hands-off message, but I was still uneasy about letting her walk the block to the project by herself.

Lily, however, was undaunted. She reigned as the *gringita* in this kingdom of adobe houses. She and Mita joked that Mita was her Mayan mother. Lily had easily made the transition from a middle-class life complete with phone, refrigerator, and television, to one whose main amenities were a cement sink in the yard and a flush toilet. And she seamlessly made friends with kids who had never ventured outside their village, or seen a lake, or eaten a pizza.

In spite of the anxieties I had had about Lily's well-being, it soon became apparent to us that the One who knows the desires of our hearts was prepared to give Lily hers.

She had always wanted a dog. I had always resisted the idea by trying to persuade her with a zoo of stuffed animals that didn't require feeding when we traveled. The village abounded in scavenger dogs. It was hard to tell which ones actually belonged to someone because none of them was as pampered or cared for as most North American pets. Perhaps it was this keen instinct for survival that caused them to recognize what a prize the *gringita* would be.

Shortly after we moved in, one dog, which actually did belong to the neighbors, jumped the four-foot-high adobe wall to get into our yard. When another sneaked in through the gate, they had a down-and-out fight. Felicidad, the neighbor's tawny, flop-eared mutt, won the day. Each day, she trailed after Lily, even to the market, where she would wait on the corner for an hour until Lily emerged.

A few months after Felicidad had adopted Lily, the dog's actual owner intercepted us on our way home and told us Felicidad was pregnant, and he had taken her to live with relatives in another town. Lily was devastated and couldn't think of enough bad things to say about him. This was great news, however, for the black-and-tan dog, which, although she had lost the fight, had never lost hope for a chance to be number one. That night I stepped out into the darkness to go to the bathroom, and there she was taking up Felicidad's old post outside the door.

But perhaps the most unlikely of God's provisions for Lily came in the form of a bodyguard—a Mayan named Marco. Barefoot, with a lazy eye, coarse black hair, and a hole in the knee of his jeans, Marco had greeted us when we first arrived at the project. He didn't actually live there but stopped by every day as he made his rounds about town.

Marco immediately attached himself to us, escorting Lily around and hanging on to Bob's every silly saying. Although he didn't speak English, he had an uncanny ability to know when Bob was making up words. "*Kakalamin*," Marco would repeat with a grin and a swagger, as though to say he understood the secret treasure of foolishness. We knew he loved being with us, and we trusted he would not hurt Lil.

When he wasn't shadowing Bob, he and Felicidad went everywhere Lily went. This often elicited perplexed looks from the more groomed Latino boys, who may have thought they were higher on the social rung for the favor of the *gringita*. And truth be told, Marco probably wasn't someone Lily would have chosen for a friend had we been in the States. But none of us were seeing things the same way anymore.

Sometimes it was difficult to picture a future and a hope for the people whose lives seemed impossibly caught in a primitive struggle for survival, but where others saw a street urchin who liked to chase after the chicken bus when it came to town, Bob saw a possibility.

Every chicken bus had an indispensable person called the *ayudante*, or helper. The *ayudante* was the one who hung out the door and decided how many inches the driver had to spare between another vehicle and the edge of the canyon. He was the one who directed the driver, otherwise blinded by people, boxes, and livestock, in critical backup maneuvers.

Every day Bob greeted Marco with, "Marco, you are the best." And, "Marco, you could be the *ayudante* on the bus when you get older. It would be a great job for you." Marco would fix his one straight eye on Bob and grin.

We had no idea that years later the Lord would show us just how powerful those words were.

10

Real Men Don't Do Dishes

*It's a noble thing to say you would lay down your life
for a loved one. It's quite another if you are called upon
unexpectedly to share your last bit of chocolate. Thank God
there is no condemnation as we slowly shed our selfish selves
and grow in grace.*

The ubiquitous firecracker shattered the silence and sent the darkness scattering into splinters of light as the new year found its way to the village. I kept my eye on Bob to see if he was going to suffer any ill effects from his outing. He and José had attended a lively church service in a neighboring village. Before he left, I reminded him not to drink anything because the villagers usually didn't boil their water. But when he saw how pleased the people were to have him as a guest, he couldn't refuse the gracious pastor who dumped the contents out of an available cup, refilled it with lukewarm coffee, and pressed it into Bob's hands.

Although we'd been very careful not to drink anything but bottled water and not eat lettuce or unpeeled fruit, we still suffered minor but frequent intestinal disorders. On one of our monthly trips to the city, we all got tested for parasites. The doctor suggested I might have amoebas and gave me a prescription. Before I bought the drug he had prescribed, I looked it up in a book I depended on, *Where There Is No Doctor*. The description was enough to send me scurrying back to the doctor.

"I don't think I'm going to take this drug," I said. "It's banned in the United States. My book lists the possible side effects as blindness, paralysis, and death."

Still defending his prescription, he replied, "That doesn't happen very often."

Being up on my Bible knowledge, I knew I had one shot at dying. I decided to take my chances on the possible amoebas (which, according to tests I had in the States months later, I did not have).

Lily and I had celebrated the New Year together at home, frothing up with RID, a treatment for head lice. Neither of us had caught any of those pesky lice that were the bane of her ability to relax; nevertheless, we felt like taking precautionary measures, and so we celebrated the passing of the year with the assurance we were nit-free.

Now I was ready to tackle that same issue that had been bugging me at the project. The kids were bemused when I pushed their heads away from mine and said I didn't want any of their *piojos*. Lice were simply an ongoing nuisance with which they lived, so they didn't understand my aversion.

Armed with my boxes of RID and little combs, I gathered everyone around the big concrete sink in the yard. I wasn't sure how they would react to my insistence on the head washings. The project had an enclosed outdoor shower, but I noticed the twins kept their clothes on when they used it for a quick rinse. I didn't know whether they were concerned about modesty, or they simply didn't like being covered with water.

One at a time, from the youngest to the oldest, they stepped forward. After I had dunked and soaped everyone's head, we waited the prescribed time for the *piojos* to die. Wearing expressions as solemn as befitted a funereal, everyone stared at each other's heads. But the sight of a dozen sudsy heads was too much for Oralia. She started giggling, and soon everyone was pointing at each other and laughing. Oralia was a good sport about humoring me, but I suspected she knew something I didn't, because even though we washed the floors, the bedding, and the clothing, we never completely eradicated those tenacious bugs.

When the kids weren't in school or working for José or one of his relatives, they came to our house. If Lily was finished with her schoolwork, they'd play ball or sit on the huge flat rock in the middle of the yard, where they'd chat and carry on, seemingly oblivious that they were speaking three different languages.

These were kids who were more familiar with work than play. These were four-foot-tall boys who by age ten carried hundred-pound sacks of corn on their backs. They did this with the aid of a *tumpline*, a leather strap that wrapped around the top of the head and attached on the back to whatever one wanted to carry. If aligned correctly, this ancient system of load-bearing was supposedly efficient. But it was not uncommon to see little boys hunched over with the strap around their foreheads, their neck muscles straining against the weight of their loads.

Tiny girls balanced smaller girls on their hips and hauled water and swept yards. Lily, whose life was tipped more on the side of play than work, had something to learn from these mini-mothers. Our teenaged twins, Julia and Blanca, were particularly good examples. They never allowed me to open a door or carry my own basket if they had an empty hand. And although I deeply appreciated their respect, I also tried to let them know they were not my servants, a role expected of many of the Mayans.

But play and laughter are also good for the soul, and at that Lily and Bob excelled. One day we set out buckets of water balloons. It didn't take long, especially after Bob joined in, and the kids realized adults were fair game, for the thrill of splatting each other with these wet bombs to escalate into a no-holds-barred war. Bob actually led the fray when he ditched his balloons for the plastic bowls I used to scoop water from the *pila*, itself a limitless supply of ammunition. Anyone passing by our gate that day might have wondered about the screams and yells and sprays of water flying over the wall. Those moments of pure fun that transcended all time and culture barriers endeared us to each other as much as any other thing we accomplished there.

Our kids did attend the public school but were years behind their grade levels. In the afternoons I helped them with their school-work and gave them Bible stories and projects to work on. Soon, so many of the neighborhood kids came by that we overflowed the table and rickety benches and spilled out onto the ever-useful straw mats on the ground.

Evita, who worked for José's wife during the day, came by in the evenings so I could teach her to read. I was usually tired after dinner, and I sometimes wondered what good my few lessons would do, but Evita looked forward to coming every night, and I didn't want to disappoint her. I think she just wanted to be around us, which was a good enough reason for me.

She lived with her mother in a simple adobe house across the street from us. I went with her one day to visit her mother, who was sick. We stepped inside the dark room. A fire pit and two mats spread on the ground defined life reduced to its most basic needs. In spite of the government billboards encouraging people to build latrines, Evita's mom, like many of the poorer people, simply used her yard, a fact I often thought about when the winds whipped the dirt and air together and blew them into my face.

Evita tried to teach me to balance a basket on my head and to carry a baby in the versatile shawl that, depending on how it was folded, became a baby sack, grocery bag, shoulder wrap, or hat. She had a curious habit of picking up a shirt or sweater I had left on a chair and burying her face in it as if to inhale my very essence. Knowing there weren't any department-store fragrances lingering in the fabric, I was appalled the first time I saw her do this. She, however, was unabashed and continued to check my scent when-ever she found my clothes lying around.

One night Evita stepped inside the gate and stopped in her tracks. "Roberto, what are you doing?" she exclaimed. Bob was standing at the *pila* washing dishes, a chore not unusual for him if I was tired.

"Washing dishes. Why?" he asked.

Evita smiled as she kindly informed him, "Men don't do dishes."

Perhaps that explained why the men who were working on a neighboring roof had stopped to watch Bob wash his breakfast dishes one morning. As Bob absorbed this bit of cultural enlightenment, he hoped Evita had forgotten about his serving-God-in-women's-underwear episode.

Living in a foreign land was not only instrumental in teaching us about other people but also in revealing our own hearts. Not having familiar places to hide behind, some of my own attitudes bared their not-so-righteous heads.

Eva Maria waited at the kitchen door for permission to enter. "*Hermana* Marcia, may I come in?"

"Certainly," I said, appreciating her manners. The kids often appeared in ones or twos and hung out in the kitchen, hoping to eat something other than beans and rice, or hoping, perhaps, to collect my empty tin cans, which they recycled into cups and cooking containers. We ate vegetables and simple boxed foods, like spaghetti or macaroni and cheese; nevertheless, our meals were special treats for kids.

"My mother wants to know if we could have some more chocolate," Eva Maria announced.

Fighting back a visceral reaction to shut the lid of the cooler in which a bag of gourmet chocolate chips lay, I stared at her. These weren't your ordinary, pick-up-at-the-store chocolates. In fact, there was no such thing as chocolate chips within hours of the village. These were a very special, unexpected gift for *me*.

We had attended an English-speaking church service in Antigua with friends who had just returned from the States. When the conversation got around to foods we missed, I mentioned how I would love some chocolate chips.

"You want chocolate chips?" my friend Ann asked. And with a flourish that rivaled a Houdini rabbit-from-the-hat trick, she reached into her bag and produced a huge sack of Ghirardelli chocolate. "Here, take it," she offered.

I couldn't believe my good fortune.

And now, here was Eva Maria, asking for more of my coveted chocolate manna. I thought I had been generous by sending a big batch of cookies over to the project the day before. Apparently, instead of satisfying their sweet tooths, I had triggered an endorphin high.

But I didn't want to share anymore. I wanted to hoard my chocolate, savor it, and parcel it out over the next few weeks. I could practically hear the little red-horned devil on one shoulder taunting the winged angel on the other.

"Lord, that's my chocolate; how rude of Oralia to send the kids over for more. There are only three of us but a dozen of them. They'll eat it all." As I listened to myself whine, I began to see there was more to this God-gift than chocolate, and what I was seeing wasn't pleasant.

Drawing the line about how much to do or how much to give was a frequent dilemma for us. People often showed up at our door looking for money, medicine, rides, or provisions. A seasoned missionary had advised us to define our primary purpose and keep it mind when faced with the constant requests. However, as I looked at Eva Maria watching me in happy anticipation, I knew this wasn't the day to argue it. The angel on my shoulder clapped her wings as I opened the cooler. "Here," I said thrusting a ziplock baggie into Eva Maria's hands.

My worldview was going totally awry here. Decisions I usually made without much forethought now piled up like a basket of laundry waiting to be sorted. I pondered each one, sorting it according to Christian, cultural, or personal response.

I had been startled, but pleased, the day I turned and saw a toothless, craggy-faced woman watching me through the open kitchen window. "It's kind of nice to be watched so much," I mused. "I can be a good Christian testimony without doing anything special, just by being myself."

But when that same old lady cut through my yard and made off with an armful of my expensive *ocote*, a resinous wood used to quick-start fires, I had yelled, "Hey," hoping to stop my thief.

"Stealing is stealing," my ethic said.

"But I have much more than she does," my conscience said.

"I am not a socialist," my analyst offered.

"No, but you are a Christian," my heart responded. By that time the woman had long gone.

The car was another source of conflict. Many of the villagers expected that since we had a vehicle, we should give rides whenever anyone wanted or needed to make the two-hour trip to the nearest city. My feelings about the road promptly settled that request. Besides, we already had to get new shocks—or at least we thought we did. It wasn't until Bob returned from having them replaced that we noticed one was black and the other was blue. When Bob returned to the shop, the mechanic looked genuinely dumbfounded. Yes, he had replaced our shocks, he said. New, to us, meant out-of-the-box new, but apparently, to our thrifty mechanic, it meant these-are-better-than-the-ones-you-have new.

Our car theoretically was designed for four people, five maximum. By Guatemalan standards that translated to at least eight, nine if someone held on outside from the step-up. There were always hitchhikers on the road, sometimes whole families going to or from the market with their goods—some of which were still kicking and squawking. But inevitably, if we stopped for one person, several more appeared from the shrubs. They would get very annoyed if we passed them by, but, I justified, they wouldn't be the ones paying for the next set of shocks or front end that I knew we'd need. But I still struggled.

Meanwhile, Bob, too, strove to keep life in perspective. One day we made the arduous trek to Guatemala City for supplies. Some friends met us, and we all went for ice cream cones. Everyone chose inexpensive, locally made ice cream, but I had my eyes on a Dove Bar—an expensive, North American chocolate Dove Bar. And that's what I ordered.

Being sensitive about our financial accountability, Bob was clearly annoyed by my extravagance. He shot me a glare that practically melted the chocolate coating right off the bar.

I hunkered down with my treat and sent a silent message back: *You've got to be kidding—I live in an adobe house, for crying out loud.*

After a short time, Bob's perspective returned, and he tried to make amends. "Marsh, I'm sorry," he apologized. "You're worth twelve Dove Bars."

Assuming he wasn't speaking literally, I accepted his apology.

11

No News, Old News, Good News

The power of God's Word does not go unnoticed. It stimulates antagonists of fear as well as recipients of faith.

The twenty-mile-long dirt road that snaked around cliffs and through rivers was our lifeline for mail and groceries and doctors. We got as excited over news about the road as a New England farmer gets about the weather. The one way in and out of town provided an endless source of discussion—someone fell over the side of one of the large trucks that could pack the population of whole villages in their wooden-slatted backs, a bus rolled over the cliff, or bandits held up a car but let the people go unharmed because the woman was pregnant.

We marveled at the types of vehicles that tackled the trek. Even the gay little ice cream truck cranked out its tinny tune as it arrived in town. Once during the dry season when the road was passable, we trailed a Pepsi truck wending its way up the mountain. At one narrow, washed-out curve, I was certain I saw the outside tires momentarily suspended in thin air.

Another time we got stuck in a traffic jam at one of the river crossings. A pickup, stalled in the middle of the river, blocked traffic from either direction. We were in a line of three or four trucks on one side. On the other, a bus topped with the usual crowd waited to cross. I thought the situation a classic commentary of life on the road and got out to take a picture.

Satisfied with my shots, I got back in the car just as an angry man stuck his face in the window and demanded to know what I was taking a picture of. Suspecting he was the owner of the stuck truck, and I must have insulted his pride, I shoved my camera under my leg and assured him I was photographing the bus. He stared me down for a minute before strutting off to rescue his vehicle.

In February, the buzz about town was that crews were working on the road. Harbingers of progress, those hulking yellow graders with their wide blades leveled the tops of ruts that had grabbed our tires and held them captive for miles. Sometimes rivulets of erosion on the drop-off side of the road ate their way into the middle part, forcing vehicles to hug the mountain wall and honk furious warnings for anyone approaching around the blind curve. With each rut smoothed over, each crevice repacked with gravel, one of my own potholes of fear was filled with new confidence. I still kept my eyes riveted on the overhanging branches and narrow passes for lurking bandits, and I still stashed our money and rings and passports around the car in case we did meet up with any gun-brandishing ill-wishers, but I began to relax enough to enjoy the beauty of the tumultuous scenery and the heartiness of the inhabitants who traveled these passes.

About twice a month we ventured out to make phone calls at one of the government-run telephone offices and to pick up our mail. Because of the unreliable government mail service, we contracted a private carrier. Originally, they had told us to pick up our mail at a store in Chichicastenego, a bustling tourist town a few hours from our village.

In the no-phone and pre-e-mail days, a letter from home was greatly anticipated. I reminded myself of a little old lady neighbor I had known, who examined each piece of her junk mail as reverently as she would a letter from the president. Now I knew how she felt. Understanding how treasured a letter from home was, I vowed to be diligent to keep in touch with missionaries when I was back in the States.

Bob found a place to park on the narrow side street near the store. We greeted the storekeeper and asked if we had mail.

"I'm sorry, not today," she said. Disappointed, we treated ourselves to lunch at one of the hotels and then returned home. Two weeks later, sure that someone had written, we again made the trip to Chichicastenego. Again, I greeted the pleasant shopkeeper, identified our mail carrier, and inquired about our mail.

Again she apologized and said, "Not today."

Frustrated, we drove to the carrier's main office, hours away in Guatemala City, where we learned they had decided to stop using that store as a drop-off location and were holding our mail for us. Although they were sure the shopkeeper knew they had stopped using her for their mail services, she apparently did not want to be the bearer of bad news. The momentary disappointment from telling someone, "Not today," was better than the upsetting finality of "never."

Although modes of communication were difficult and intermittent, neither rutted roads, nor bandits, nor unreliable mail carriers could prevent one testosterone-riddled ritual—the Super Bowl.

Super Bowl Sunday arrived in the village on a February night. Our friend Tim had sworn all his ham radio contacts to silence about the outcome of the January game because his mother in Minnesota was going to tape it and send the cassette with a couple who planned to visit Tim and Dena the following month. Although we suspected Dallas had beaten the Buffalo Bills, none of the ham contacts breathed a word over the airwaves during the month it took for the video to arrive.

On the long-awaited day, we all gathered in the living room. After dinner, Dena made popcorn. Tim put the video in the VCR.

Soon into the game, Dallas took the lead. The Bills responded with a touchdown.

A knock at the front door interrupted the football chatter. Dena answered it, and after a brief discussion with the man outside, walked in front of the TV screen, retrieved something from her medical supplies, and went outside again.

Two minutes later Dena returned and settled back into her chair. "Hector stepped on a nail. I had to give him a tetanus shot," she said. Tim simply nodded as though this were as normal an interruption as a commercial. Then he whooped as Dallas retrieved the ball.

In the next instant the television screen crackled as the Dallas Cowboys imploded into a tiny central speck of light. Overhead bulbs popped and died out. We sat in silent darkness. Someone went to the window and concluded, "The whole town is out. The guerrillas must have blown a transformer."

Not about to let this most-important-male-moment be thwarted by a disruptive rebel group, Tim quickly assessed his options. "I'll get the generator."

Designating the refrigerator and the TV the two most important recipients of the electricity, the men connected the wires, and the Super Bowl exploded back to life.

As I sat there, I imagined what it would look like if I could hover in the darkness above the village and observe the only speck of light for miles around, flickering from a television set at the home of the gringos as they cheered their football teams on to a victory long won.

During the short time we had been in the village, we were so focused at the project that we hadn't visited many of the *aldeas*—the tiny, neighboring mountain communities. Bob longed to share the hope of Christ with the people who burned candles on the stone altars dotting the hillsides and whose ancestors believed they had come from corn. So he was overjoyed when one of the Christian teachers from town who assisted the Bible translator suggested they go to an unreached mountain community where Bob could share the gospel.

The three of them arrived in the remote village just before dusk. A cluster of people sat on the concrete porch under the roofed overhang of the school building.

Bob spoke a few sentences in English, which the Bible translator repeated in Spanish for the teacher, who then translated them into the local dialect. Like spectators at a slow-motion tennis match, the small group watched the words pass down the line from one speaker to the next and then back again. It was a tedious process, but the people were curious and attentive.

Without the benefit of electricity, darkness settled quickly in the folds of mountains. Bob was momentarily distracted by a line of small round lights snaking up the trail toward the gathering. As he continued to preach, several somber men silently took a place in the front row. They shut off their flashlights and listened as Bob told the group about a God who loved and set free and gave hope and eternal life. When he finished, the row of latecomers rose, flicked on their flashlights, and filed back down the mountain as silently as they had come.

A few people stayed to speak with Bob's friends and receive prayer. But one man said he was afraid of what the tribal leaders would think.

The next day, the Bible translator told Bob they had received a warning. The tribal leaders, perhaps the shaman, had spoken: the gospel bearers had better not return to their *aldea*—or else.

Christians in town had a lot of liberty to share their faith.

They could hang a sheet on the walls of buildings near the park and show the *Jesus* film to the whole town without reprisal, but white men invading these dark, distant hills with talk about the light of Jesus were another matter.

12

Demonic Cows, Ailing Livers, and Ample Provisions

Sometimes it is simply best to be still and know that he is God.

Although all the churches I attended in the States affirmed their belief in the reality of the spirit world, few actually entertained the possibility of a physical manifestation of angels or demons breaking into their tidy idea of reality. Spirit beings, like proper children at a dinner table, were present but not heard. But the people of these highlands didn't know that. Life here was steeped in the reality of the spirit world.

I wasn't privy to what went on in the Mayan temple or in the secluded hillsides. What was most visible were the rituals in which Mayan deities merged with Catholic saints. Traditional Christian celebrations, interwoven with ancient beliefs and a generous dose of alcohol, formed the warp and woof of a religious tapestry suited more for tourism than for salvation. The processions of idols, the incessant chants, and the wax-soaked altars drenched the air and disturbed our spirits.

The space between the natural and the supernatural was stretched thin. So many people, including other missionaries, had told us stories about apparitions, demons, and supernatural happenings that I found myself on the lookout for shadowy things lurking in the edges of my vision. That's probably why I reacted so to the cow.

Dena showed up at our door one morning and said Tim was sick and needed to get to a doctor in Guatemala City. They had made radio contact with Mission Aviation Fellowship, which was sending a plane. She asked if we could drop them off at the airport and stay with Caleb and Nathan for a few days.

Dena is one of those people who approaches life very calmly. I scrambled to interpret all the information she had just delivered. I knew they would not take Tim's sickness lightly because of the complications of his paralysis. I also knew if they thought it was serious enough for him to be flown out, we would not hesitate to help. What I was surprised about was the mention of an airport. In all the time we had lived in the village, I had never seen an airplane or anything that resembled an airport.

We met at their house. Tim was weak but managed to scoot himself in the front seat of our SUV. Bob stashed the wheelchair in the cargo space, and the rest of us piled in the backseat. Dena had packed some overnight bags. They had to travel light because of the weight constrictions for takeoff and landing, and she wanted to save room to bring back supplies. Tim directed us down a dirt road in a part of town I had never explored.

"There it is," he said. "Park here outside the fence."

I don't know what I expected, but a barbed wire fence surrounding a cow pasture was not it. We heard the muted drone of a small plane in the distance. It appeared over the hill, circled the field, and lined up for a landing. Someone shooed the cows away. Tim told us it was the Mennonite pastor from town. "Whenever the plane wants to land, it circles the town to signal the pastor, who jumps on his motorcycle and gets here in time to clear the cows."

"So how will we know when to pick you up?" I asked.

"The pilot will circle the village a few times to let you know when we return," Dena said.

Within minutes of loading Tim and Dena into the little Cessna, the pilot bumped down the grassy runway, tipped his wings, and disappeared over the southern hills.

Since it was easier for us to move over to Tim and Dena's house than to move the twins in with us, we collected our belongings and drove to the north end of town. Tim and Dena had moved from their home across from the market to a new house that had been built on the outskirts of the village. The owner had built the house himself. Knowing he would be renting to Tim, he had incorporated certain wheelchair-friendly features they requested, such as an easily-accessible tiled tub. An iron-gated wall separated the front yard from the dirt road leading out of town.

I was sitting on the front porch so I could keep my eye on Caleb and Nathan, who were jumping off a plastic slide. It was late afternoon. In the distance a billowing dust cloud followed after a herd of cows as they returned from the day in the upper meadows. They thundered down the street, the heat from their bodies distorting the waves of afternoon light. I watched as they passed by our gate, which was closed but not bolted.

The cows were wide-eyed, hot, and intent on getting home. One, in particular, was frothing heavily at the mouth. As the herd continued on, she pulled aside and stopped in front of our yard. I ran to the gate and waved my arms to shoo her away, but she didn't budge. Bubbles of foam dripped off her lips.

Was she just hot, or did she have rabies? I wondered. People from the health department periodically drove through the village with megaphones mounted on their cars, inviting pet owners to vaccinate their pets. But did that include cows?

Yelling for Caleb and Nathan to get inside, I struggled to secure the bolt. The cow stood on the other side, her flared nostrils pushed against the gate. She was determined to come in. I managed to slide the bolt into place and ran into the house with the kids. We peeked out the window. She was still there, panting and foaming, her gaze fixed on our gate.

I was already feeling that extra sense of responsibility that comes with living in someone else's house and caring for their children. On top of which, I was concerned about Lily, who had woken up that morning with a fever. Now I had this insistent bovine at my gate.

This is definitely not normal behavior for a cow, I thought. Chills skittered down my arms as another possibility occurred to me. *It's demonic.* Huddling my little charges around me, I started to pray. Relieved, we watched as the cow eventually abandoned her post and ambled down the road.

Tim and Dena had been gone a couple of days when we heard the distant low hum of an engine. We ran outside to see the plane make several wide loops around the village, giving us time to drive to the field. Happy to see both of them exit the plane, we piled into the car and awaited their report.

"Tim has hepatitis," Dena said. "We think one of the boys had a mild case, which we didn't notice. When we washed his diapers, some water must have splashed back into the reservoir of the *pila* and polluted it. A couple of other people who ate at our house are also sick."

We all looked at Lily, who by this time was vomiting and listless. As Dena helped Tim into bed, I told them about the demonic cow. Tim laughed.

"That cow belongs to the man who built this house," he said. "He used to feed it here every afternoon. It was just looking for dinner."

Not able to defend the idea of a cow possessed of a hunger demon, I simply shrugged. Who knew people kept pet cows?

We decided to leave first thing in the morning to get Lily to the doctor in Antigua. As it turned out, arrangements had already been made for us long before we even knew we had a need.

The last time we had been in Antigua, our friends Dan and

Ann offered us use of their spacious apartment while they were in the States. We had thanked them for the offer but said we didn't expect to be in the city during that time.

"I'll tell you where the key is anyway," Ann said. "We'll let the owners of the property know in case you change your minds."

A month later, unexpectedly finding ourselves in need of a place to stay until Lily got better, we were appreciative of their foresight to leave the key. Little did we know that stopover would turn into weeks, as we all succumbed to hepatitis.

The stone building they rented was carved alongside some ancient ruins in the back corner of an estate. The familiar masses of orange and magenta flowers cascaded over the high wall that enclosed the whole compound. Gardeners tended the lush gardens and fruit trees. It was a quiet tropical paradise within a stone's throw of the market. Not only would we be able to get fresh food, but since the property had its own well and purification system, we would be able to have good water and flush toilets.

I didn't know why God didn't prevent us from getting sick, but I was thankful for how he provided such a beautiful and convenient haven where we could recover.

It was late in the day by the time we arrived in town and found a doctor. He prodded Lily's enlarged liver. The whites of her eyes had turned yellow, and her urine was the color of cola. She not only had hepatitis A but also a urinary infection, which the doctor did not want to treat with drugs because they would be metabolized by the already stressed liver. There was no treatment for the hepatitis, he said, except rest and time.

"Eat fruits and vegetables but absolutely no fats," he ordered.

A week later, as Lily's eyes turned from yellow back to white, and energy returned to her lethargic body, Bob came down with a fever. Although this type of hepatitis sucks the life essence right out of your body, it is not fatal—a fact Bob refused to believe. After being in the clutches of sickness for several days, he dragged himself out of bed and plunked a chair down in the middle of the room. He sat there shirtless, with the fan aimed straight at him, and stared vacantly at the cassette player, which was playing a praise tape.

"I'm dying," he said.

"No, you are not," I countered. "Look how much better Lily is, and she had a urinary tract infection on top of it."

"I have it worse," he stated, his flat monotone attesting to the lack of life force left in his body. He hadn't moved anything except for his lips. An hour later he was still there, immobile, waiting for the last wisp of breath to exit his body. I called some men we knew from the church to come and pray and prod him back to the land of the living.

A few days later Bob got out of bed, and I crawled in. But my days spent staring out the window from between the sheets were cut short by a convergence of factors that forced our decision about our remaining time in Guatemala.

Part Two

Going

I know God likes order. He has, after all, arranged pinecones and sunflowers and nautilus shell spirals in tidy Fibonacci number patterns, and has ordered the earth to orbit the sun in a predictable time that accommodates our calendars.

But sometimes he confounds us by throwing in a platypus, or strewing the night sky with garlands of wavy colors, or hiding 96 percent of the matter of the universe from prying eyes.

His ways are mysterious and marvelous. And they are often altogether more uncomfortable, more uncertain, and more unnerving than my own. But because I believe he is who he says he is, and that he cares for me, I have committed to trust him, to see the "evidence of things unseen," even in the darkness when there is no response to my "Why?"

13

Leave Your Orphans Behind

Although I say, "Of course I believe," when heaven parts
and pins me in the spotlight of the Living One Who Sees
Me, I am brought to my knees in awe.

It was mid-March. Our car's visa was due to expire on April 6. Since we hadn't wanted to pay the thousands of dollars to register it, every six months we had to remove it from the country for a period of thirty days. People had figured out ways to get around this. Some drove out of the country at one border and crossed back in from another. We didn't want to try that, but considered another option, which involved driving twelve hours to a hotel in Mexico that, for a fee, would let us park our car in their secure lot for the month. We would then have to take the bus back to the village and live without a vehicle for a month, then take the bus back to Mexico, retrieve our car, and drive back to the village.

The thought of doing all this when we were well was dismal enough, but to have to consider it when the hepatitis had left us with about as much energy as a sloth on sedatives was impossible. Nevertheless, we may have chosen to do it if we weren't already weary on another front.

For the past several weeks, frustrations, like a school of minnows after bread crumbs, had nibbled at our peace and taken bites out of our effectiveness. Some of the problems arose from differences about work ethics (to be sure, our *today* attitude had a hard time submitting to the popular *mañana* one). Other conflicts revolved around money and accountability. Whenever we thought we were caught up with the past debts, a new one would appear.

Bob was not wired to be a maintenance man, but because the ministry didn't have a local governing board, he was hesitant to seek more aggressive sources of support that would generate funds. It's not that we doubted anyone's sincere intentions to provide a haven for widows and orphans, but because it was a privately run ministry, we thought a local board a good idea. When Bob suggested that there were a few people in town he thought would be willing to serve on such a board, he was told to simply trust God.

Apparently they believed in the feasibility of a pure heart, but we were only too aware of our own shortcomings to trust someone else's. As I watched Bob's growing frustration, a wad of anxiety settled in the pit of my stomach. The dreaded possibility that we might have to reconsider our options, rebuild our raft, hovered in the background of my mind and stared at me in the early morning hours.

This was very distressing. I didn't want to rip up our new roots so soon. My thoughts cast about like fragile tendrils looking for something to curl around and anchor to. I crept into the kitchen in the still-dark morning hours to pray—especially for Bob, because in spite of the popular Southern saying, "If momma ain't happy, ain't nobody happy," I had long ago suspected that I could be content anywhere as long as my husband was at peace. "Be anxious for nothing . . ." I penned in my journal day after day.

Although the kids continued to come over every day, and we worked with Oralia on the meals, we had lost momentum. Each of us harbored the unspoken conclusion that our days at the project were numbered, but without a clear idea of what we should do, we continued on in the energy-sapping land of indecision.

I don't know how many times a day God gets asked, "What should I do? Where should I go?" Although he's not too fond of the pillar-of-cloud-by-day-and-pillar-of-fire-by-night approach anymore, the Bible tells us that he does still direct our paths and show us the way. Consequently, we, in our efforts to understand, list options like answers on a multiple-choice test for God to choose from. We look for "doors to open" and "doors to close," and we drive ourselves silly with worry that we'll miss the turn or not recognize his direction.

Whenever I started getting too frantic about change and choice, I thought back to the first advice I recognized as coming straight from the Lord to me when I was a brand-new believer and had run out of places to live. I was holing up in the nursery of my very first church. Deciding it was time for a serious talk with God, I stationed myself on the couch and declared I would not move until he gave me some direction. I sat, and I waited. After a while I saw in my mind's eye, much like a banner streaming from an airplane over an ocean beach, "Be still and know that I am God."

I started to dismiss it with "What kind of an answer is that? I know you're God." But, instead, I was drawn into the center of understanding that if I truly believed he was *God*, there was no reason to be so frantic. A few minutes later I got up from that couch and knew exactly what I had to do.

So that was the truth I focused on as the mild Guatemalan winter gave way to spring—practicing calm trust in the midst of indecision. The deciding factor arrived in the mail. Our tenants back in New Jersey had been transferred out-of-state and requested to break their lease. The hepatitis, the car's visa, the disheartened vision, and the tenants—all tangled together. With heavy hearts, we decided to leave the village and return to the States.

Lily surprised me when we told her. I expected her to be overjoyed about going home, but she registered the news in silence; conflicting shadows of anticipation and sadness flitted across her face. Later, I picked up a paper on which she had been drawing. There were two round yellow faces. The first one had a big open mouth and was screaming, "Noo!" The second was smiling. She captioned it "Guatemala! Here we come! At first I hated it, but soon I learned to love it!"

The effusive welcome Mita, Oralia and the kids gave us when we returned to the village from our sick stay in Antigua only deepened my sense of betrayal. I didn't know how to tell them we would be leaving for good in a few weeks. I wasn't as worried about Oralia as I was Mita. Oralia was a woman of great strength and ambition. She and her children were ready to move back to her husband's village. Mita cried. She worried about how well she and her children would be taken care of once we left if no one replaced us promptly.

Bob and I had already discussed the possibility of helping Mita financially if she chose to leave the project and get her own place in town. We pledged to give her enough money to cover her rent and food for a year while she worked on some means of support. We had arranged to leave the money with a reliable person in town who would oversee her monthly payments.

I had no idea how Mita would handle this decision. She had been dependent on others for a long time, and I didn't know if she was even capable of envisioning a future as an independent woman or if she had the courage to walk away from the project. But she was the one who would have to live out the consequences of her decision, and she was the one who had to make it. Anticipating that she might not be able to decide until she saw what happened after we left, I reassured her, "You don't have to decide right now. We will leave some money for you before we go in case you decide later."

It was the week before Easter. Although Antigua was world famous for its religious processions and pageantry, our village held its own claim to fame among the mountain communities. For days, the streets feeding into the town square burgeoned with seekers and spectators as cultural and religious customs collided in an explosion of color, music, processions, and parties. On Thursday, the turquoise bus waited on the corner as barefoot Mayan men carried huge green-and-red-painted crosses in a solemn procession through town. Throughout the day the town buzzed with festive anticipation.

At night we went to a basketball tournament in the central plaza. I slowly turned in a circle to take in the kaleidoscope of unrelated activities occurring all around the plaza. The Black Saints basketball team outshot their rivals at one end of the square while young boys chased a soccer ball in the other end. Mayan men chanted on the church steps where a Judas effigy hung from the scaffolding. Clusters of women in ceremonial headdress, enterprising stray dogs, and men on horseback making their way through the crowd added to the discordant celebration.

We went back down to town on Good Friday to watch the sufferers—men who had fasted up in the mountains—crawl through town, their faces covered with cloth secured by a crown of thorns, another ball of long thorns piercing their backs. They stopped in front of pine-branch-covered shrines, I supposed, to offer up prayers of penance. The drums, the chants, the prayers, and the drinking continued late into the night.

On Easter Sunday, the town was quiet.

Although I was no longer contagious with hepatitis, I still had not recovered my strength and tired easily. One morning, I lay back down on the bed shortly after I had gotten up. We were leaving in two days. I knew I had much to do to finish packing, but I was too depressed to begin.

"What was this all about, Lord?" I cried. "It seems so pointless to have gone through so much turmoil and energy to get here only to leave a few months later. I feel like all we've done is tutor a few kids, clean cow poop, and pay bills. Now Mita and her kids depend on us, and we're going to leave them. Please show me that all this wasn't a waste—that it mattered to someone."

Blanca, the quiet twin, stood at the door and waited for permission to enter. I motioned her in and patted a place on the bed beside me. She picked up some papers I had collected for the kids to color and began stapling them. No one spoke. We had come a long way in crossing borders of understanding, this little teenage Mayan girl with the long braid and big eyes, and me, the pale, weak, middle-aged gringa. For the next hour, our hearts just hovered there together in the quiet exchange of each other's presence.

Like the call of the animals to Noah's ark, an unannounced parade of people arrived one by one at the door. After Blanca left, Eva Maria popped in. She gave me a salt-dried gourd bowl. "My grandmother made it," she declared proudly. It was the first time someone from the village, other than a North American, had given me a gift. I remembered all the times Eva Maria had annoyed me—calling in the gate at 7:00 a.m. to ask if we were having pancakes; fetching my prized chocolate; tagging along with us, her high-pitched voice enthusiastically commenting on everything; and fussing over the shoes we had bought because one was more faded than the other. I hugged her in deep appreciation.

Sweet, undemanding little Mary peeked in and asked how I was. She was trailed by eight-year-old Alberto, a boy from town who came to our school and Bible study. "I'll miss you," he said. "I don't have many friends."

Throughout the day, various people stopped by, smiled, asked how I was, and expressed their friendship. I should have been overjoyed by this response, but as much as I appreciated it, I got more depressed. Halfheartedly, I propped up my pillow and opened my Bible.

Usually if I am looking for encouragement from the Lord, I

read from Isaiah—the last half, the one with the happy promises—or from Hebrews, two of my favorite books. But this time, for no reason other than his reputation as the weeping prophet, I turned to Jeremiah. After a few minutes my eyes stopped as though held by an invisible magnetic force at the bottom of page 770. The passage was too precise, too personal to doubt. It was also so unusual; I knew I had never subconsciously filed it away.

Cushioned in a silent moment of awe, I held my breath as the Creator of the universe comforted me on my sickbed in a tiny Mayan village:

> Leave your orphans behind, I will keep them alive;
> And let your widows trust in Me. (Jeremiah 49:11)

14

The Other Side of the River

When this life doesn't make sense, it's good to
remember you are just traveling through.

B ob shut the door of our house for the last time, strapped Lily's bike to the Sears cargo carrier on top of the car, and drove up to the project, where everyone was gathered. Our hugs held no concern about lice as we pressed dear faces to our cheeks. Just as she had months earlier, Oralia looked me straight in the eye, but instead of asking, "When are you coming to stay?" she asked, "When are you coming back?"

My response rang as hollow as stone in a tin can. "Soon, I hope."

Marco held the gate open as we backed out, his sorrow trickling down his face. The black-and-tan dog, sensing this wasn't an ordinary trip to town, chased our dust cloud so far down the road we had to stop and, in spite of our own heavy hearts, throw stones at her to go back.

For the first time in all our months in the village, we met the chicken bus coming toward us on the narrow road. The *ayudante* jumped out and checked the clearance. Confident his driver could make it, he waved him forward. I looked out my window at the sheer drop. If I opened my door and stepped out, I'd be walking on air. The bus crept toward us. Although what I saw defied my rational mind, I had lived in this country long enough to know that they would indeed pass by with inches to spare. The group on top of the bus leaned over and watched with great interest as the bus squeezed past. I exhaled, turned, and waved my last good-bye to the people of the village that captured my heart.

It was a dangerous day to be traveling. We stopped to buy the paper. The glaring headline of the *Prensa Libre* reported 130 people had been implicated in the beating of a North American woman. She was taking pictures of some children in a park and someone suspected her of planning to kidnap them. It was fear incarnate as a vicious mob rendered the woman unconscious.

We had known the indigenous people were suspicious of North Americans, and, consequently, had treasured our small advances into their communities. But rumors traveled far and reached into the mountain valleys that wouldn't see telephone wires for years to come. North Americans were suspected of stealing children to sell them or their body parts. When I first heard this, I thought it another unfounded suspicion prevalent among unsophisticated people. I tried to tell Mita it wasn't true, but she had been adamant—people did steal their children and their parts.

Now, years later, sadder with more knowledge of the evils of life, I suspect there was more truth to the matter than I realized.

Although we left Guatemala on the lookout for dangers as we had six months earlier when we arrived, we approached the Guatemalan/Mexican border with far more mettle than we had on that previous crossing. Bob wore a confidence hewn out of experience as he slowed for the expected interrogation. The official suspended his stamp above our papers and informed us how much he liked Lily's bike.

Bob smiled. "It's our daughter's," he said. "She likes it too."

The official was in a good mood. He stamped our papers and wished us well.

As we sailed through Mexico, we marveled at how much better the roads were than they had been earlier. Filled potholes and paved shoulders made us wonder what had changed more in six months—the roads or us. Nevertheless, as before, it was difficult to gauge traveling time and plan overnight stops. The second day on the road we had hoped to make Veracruz, but after nine hours of driving, Bob was exhausted. We stopped at what appeared to be a typical tourist town nestled on the side of a lake ringed by volcanoes.

The tourists, we discovered, were hardly typical. Most had headed back to the hills after recently concluding their annual convention, a yearly gathering of *brujos*—the sorcerers, shamans, witches, and assorted healers. We drove up and down the streets, past pink-painted shops that sold devil trinkets, herbs, and spells. I set out my spiritual antenna and tried to get a reading on whether to stay or to take our chances on the night highway.

Bob saw a hotel that had an enclosed compound for our car. Clinging to the assurance that *"Greater is he who is in me than he who is in the world,"* we checked in. The air was heavy with humidity. Lily paused to watch a happy Mexican family on holiday play in the packed pool. Several chunky boys, fully clad, splashed and dunked each other. She decided to pass on a swim. We got a bite to eat and went to bed.

It was pitch-dark, but something had woken me. I sat up, disoriented from troubling dreams that lurked just outside my recall. Suddenly, Lily sat up and bolted out of bed.

"I'm going to throw up."

We scooted to the tiny bathroom. I held back her hair, and she continued to heave long after anything remained; then I pushed her aside as my innards emptied their contents. The nausea abated as quickly as it had come, and we both lapsed into a restless sleep. The next morning, long before the other guests were up and about, an empty parking space betrayed our hasty departure. (Later, I found out that my sister in New York, who had no idea where we were at the time, had woken up that same night we were in the town of the sorcerers, with an urgency to pray for us.)

Three days later, still several miles from the Reynosa-Hidalgo border crossing, we got as fidgety as first-grade boys in the bathroom line. I totally understood what the poet William Shenstone meant when he said, "The proper means of increasing the love we bear for our native country is to reside some time in a foreign one." I couldn't wait to get back to the country where I could drive my car without threat of bribes and bandits, where I could go to the Pizza Hut without greeting an armed guard, where I didn't experience fear and oppression on every outing.

By the time we arrived, we were so excited to see the huge American flag in the distance that we crossed into the United States without turning in our exit papers on the Mexican side, an oversight which meant the Mexican government could charge a hefty fee to our credit card.

Bob was not giving up his purchase of American soil so easily. "We can cancel the card," he declared in a moment of defiance. "I am not turning around." I gave him my most sympathetic *You have to* gaze. Reluctantly, he made the U-turn back across the border. An hour later, properly stamped, we once again set our faces on that red, white, and blue beckoning us on the other side of the river.

Our tears, like the muddy waters of the Rio Grande below us, marked yet another border crossing as the heaviness about what we left behind merged with the anticipation of what we would encounter ahead.

Part Three

Full Circle

SOME THINGS CAN'T BE SEEN BY LOOKING AT THEM HEAD-ON. Like a dim star in a dark sky. At first glance it appears to be there, but when you stare at the spot, it disappears. Then, just as you turn your head away, it reappears in your peripheral vision. It was really there all along; you just had to change your perspective to catch it.

Following faith through the disappointments, doubts, and delays of life requires latching on to things unseen, believing that even when the path takes a seeming detour, the One you've pinned your hope on is faithful and true. And he's going to be right there, reminding you as he did the fretting Martha, *"Did I not say to you, if you believe, you will see the glory of God?"* (John 11:40).

15

Dried-Up Dreams

When you've lost sight of his tracks, go back to the point last seen and set your marker: this far God has met me.

I wore the year following our return from Guatemala as though it were a lead apron on my chest. We moved back into our New Jersey home. Bob returned to his job in the electrical union, dutifully leaving at 4:00 a.m. for the daily commute to New York City two hours away. Lily donned baggy jeans and preteen concerns without missing a beat. The only apparent remnant of her foreign life was the long hair-wrap she had acquired that first day on a sidewalk in Antigua.

The ripples from the boulder that had been tossed into my pond ebbed away, and life resumed as though it had never been interrupted—except for the vague depression, the persistent ennui, and the loss of direction that dogged my every move—except for the knowledge that something big *had* displaced the waters of my life and was still there under the surface.

I wondered what Mita and Julia and Blanca and Marco were doing as I slipped through the portal of my world thousands of miles away. It had been so intense; we had been so sure we were following God, but now all we had were fading pictures stuck in an album.

I even felt teary when we traded in the sturdy SUV that had carried us through three countries, forded rivers and rutted roads, and brought us safely back again. Under its hood, patches of the red dust of the village clung to the engine crevices. The carpet still bore the poop stains from hauling José's chickens. "It's just a car," I scolded myself. "Why on earth are you weepy about a machine?"

But it wasn't just a machine. It was my last link with a people and place that had uprooted my complacency and captured my heart.

As I slogged through my days, I strove to understand what the journey to Guatemala had been about. I still had no idea why we had gone, only to return after so short a time with so little apparent accomplishment.

My theology presupposed a God of relationship and communication. After all, the Bible was full of wondrous accounts performed for the sole purpose that people would know him. It was therefore reasonable, I thought, to expect him to communicate with me and to expect me to be able to recognize that communication. Now, confusion clouded the previous intimate encounters, and niggling demons of doubt threatened to make off with my confidence. Knowing God wasn't a god of whimsy and capriciousness to toss us to and fro, I questioned whether he had even spoken to us in the first place. Had we been faithful or foolish? That's what I wanted to know.

Everything in me said, "Go back." I enjoyed Spanish colonial architecture; I could eat tortillas, beans, and rice every day. I loved the soft nuances of the language and wanted to learn it more. But mostly, my heart was stuck with a little band of friends in a remote Mayan highland village. And so I plotted and planned how we could return to Central America.

We considered buying a small house stateside, in a place like Florida, where we wouldn't have to worry about freezing pipes if we left it empty for several months out of the year while we did some sort of short-term missions in Central America. This was the daydream I was occupied with one summer afternoon when the phone rang. It was my brother Mike, in Vermont. After hemming and hawing for a few minutes, he got down to it.

"Marsh, I know how odd this sounds," he began. "But I was out on my lawn tractor, thinking about my church, how we haven't had a pastor in over a year and we're down to eight families. Now one of them just called to say they were thinking about leaving.

"Well,"—he hesitated—"I know you're probably not interested, but I just felt like I had to call Bob. I know he's wanted to go into the ministry, and, well, I was wondering if he'd be interested in coming here."

It took a few minutes for that bit of information to make its way into my consciousness, but then, with a speed of a fighter jet locked on target, neurons scrambled into action against the intruder of my plans. My dream of a stucco house with a clay-tiled roof reared up against images of smoky chimneys on roofs buried under a foot of snow. Thoughts of living with people who said, *"Yup,"* instead of, *"Sí,"* living with freezing cold instead of balmy sunshine, upended the peaceful places in my mind. I processed, evaluated, and rejected the idea on the spot.

Absolutely not. I was going south, not north. Besides, how on earth could eight families support us? I suspected it wasn't as easy to go without money in the United States as it was in a rural village in Central America.

But once again, a providential plan had already been put into place that would overturn my own. I heard myself say, "Wow. I don't know, but *as it happens*, we are taking Lily to Camp Tapawingo in the Adirondacks next weekend. It's only a couple of hours from you. Maybe we can swing by after dropping her off, and Bob can preach on Sunday." I spent the rest of the day weighing this potential turn of events. Here I was, once again grappling with the dilemma of conflicting dreams between husband and wife. Early in our marriage, we had jockeyed to sort out our roles. I was a brand-new Christian at the time, and although happy to become a "kept woman," I was leery about the submission part I'd heard went with the word *wife*.

My city husband had seemed a little uncertain about the idea that his new bride came with her own nail apron, but soon realized the benefits of a handy woman far outweighed any threat to his manhood. Eventually, respect for each other's gifts and trust in each other's judgment settled most of our decisions. Now, although comfortable with my own independence, I did defer to his leadership.

I wanted to support him in whatever it seemed God was calling him to do, and I certainly didn't want to stand before the Lord someday and try to whimper out some excuses why I hadn't, but a detour to the North didn't seem like a reasonable way for God to finish what he started when he planted a heart for missions in me.

Going to Guatemala had required courage I didn't think I had, but this move would cost me my dreams. I couldn't understand why God would want something for a husband that was so contrary to the hopes of his wife. Besides, my doubts about being missionary material paled in comparison with what I felt about having pastor's wife qualifications. This time there was no place in my mind for compromise. By the time Bob came home, I knew exactly what I was going to say.

"We got a curious phone call from my brother Mike today. You know that little country church he goes to? A lot of families have left because they haven't had a pastor for the past year. He wanted to know if you'd be interested in preaching sometime. I said we'd be in the area next week and you'd probably enjoy filling in on Sunday." And with amazing aplomb, this God-fearing woman left out the other half of the phone discussion—the half about preaching on Sundays permanently.

Bob was delighted to have an opportunity to share God's Word. He spent the week preparing his sermon. I was miserable. I spent the week arguing with the Lord. I knew I would lose, but I gave it my most stubborn Yankee try. Before the week was out, I broke the news to Bob that actually the church was looking for more than a guest preacher. I scowled as the light of possibilities flickered in his eyes.

Meanwhile, taking an idea from the biblical story of Gideon, who put a fleece of wool on the threshing floor and told the Lord if the fleece was damp with dew in the morning but the floor dry, he would know for certain the Lord had spoken, I decided to set out my own fleece. I didn't tell anyone about the strange idea that occurred to me.

I told God that if I heard anyone speaking Spanish the weekend we were in Vermont, I would take it as a sign of reassurance that even if I let go of my hopes and dreams of returning to Central America, all would be well.

Later, when I reflected on my request, I realized how absurd it was. Out of the two thousand or so people who lived in the greater Clarendon area, about seven were Hispanic. The chances of running into them in those spread-out hills and dales were pretty slim—especially since we were going to be there only one night. The church itself wasn't even in an actual town. It bordered a sheep pasture on one side and an ancient cemetery on the other.

The only fleece I was going to be seeing would be walking around on four legs, I chided myself.

16

The Fleece

There is no complaint or fear or hidden place in my heart that he is not aware of. By faith, I present my concerns and choose not to fret and stew.

Leaving Lily comfortably ensconced in her island cabin, we threaded our way down the winding mountain route into the bustling tourist town of Lake George and crossed the border from New York into Vermont. It was a gloriously idyllic Vermont day, as those brief summer days are—blue skies, billowy clouds, and green fields dotted with Vermont's familiar black-and-white Holstein cows.

When we arrived in Clarendon, Mike's wife, Georgie, had dinner ready. Knowing my penchant for strawberry-rhubarb pie, she had pulled a homemade one from the freezer. After catching up on family news, Mike shared how bad he felt that after 170 years as a house of worship and an iconic community gathering place for potluck dinners and strawberry festivals, the church was down to a handful of families, struggling to keep it going. He looked at Bob hopefully.

I helped Georgie with the dishes and prepared for bed. No one had spoken a word that by any stretch of the imagination could be construed as sounding like *gracias* or *amigo*.

The eight-hundred-pound bell in the belfry clanged out its summons to any who were lingering over the morning paper or, worse yet, slumbering under the covers. The gravel parking lot bustled with activity. Children huddled by the barbed-wire fence and tried to coax the sheep with fistfuls of grass. Long-absent members showed up to check out the potential pastor, who, as the grapevine announced, was younger than ones typical in the church's history, and who even had a family.

The historic brick building, complete with steeple and fragile ,painted-glass windows, sat on land where Ethan Allen and his Green Mountain Boys had once trod (and probably bled) less than a half century before its construction. In the entryway, a display of ceramic spittoons, once stationed at the ends of the pews, was now safely locked behind glass doors. Antique couches and chairs lined the altar behind the pulpit. An organ and a piano were squeezed in a back corner. I chose a pew in the front, careful to see if anyone cast a wary eye. Members had long-standing pew-sitting habits, but I doubted that included the front-row ones.

One glance at the bulletin told me that this congregational system, which traced its roots back to the *Mayflower*, was going to be as foreign an experience for us as our first service in Guatemala had been. We were used to independent Bible fellowships located in unpretentious, renovated buildings. The services generally followed a simple format of contemporary worship followed by a sermon.

Quiet chatter ceased as the organist, a Seventh-Day Adventist, who, because she attended church on Saturday, was available to play here on Sunday, pumped out the first chord. The choir opened with a choral call to worship, followed by a hymn, Psalter reading, Gloria Patri, announcements, Lord's Prayer, offering, and doxology. After much sitting and standing, Bob was introduced.

He stepped to the front and placed his Bible on the lectern. His distinct Brooklyn accent echoed off the 170-year-old walls as he delivered a message of God's faithfulness from the book of Ruth. The image of Ruth gleaning the leftovers in the fields after the workers seemed particularly relevant as I read the rest of the bulletin, which included the weekly offering and the attendance. Sixteen people had attended service the previous Sunday. The average weekly offering was $171.00.

How on earth can they afford us? I again wondered. A quotation under the rummage sale news caught my eye: *"Faith is the brave endeavor, the splendid enterprise, the strength to serve, whatever conditions may arise."* Properly chastised, I stood for the closing hymn, "In My Life, Lord, Be Glorified," and the postlude.

After the service we headed to the back hall for coffee before leaving for our long drive back to Jersey. My brother Mike had ridden to the church with us, so I crawled in the backseat for the short ride to his house. Bob started the engine but paused to look at the sheep gazing at him on the other side of the fence.

I thought about my fleece and chuckled. "We have about thirty more seconds in this town, Lord," I said under my breath. "That was really a wild thing to ask you to do."

Just as Bob was about to shift into reverse, an older-model, maroon Ford LTD pulled alongside. An elderly, perfectly groomed woman stepped out. Mike rolled down his window and greeted her. "Why, hello, Mrs. Howard."

She smiled at him and then extended her arm through the car window to me in the backseat. Taking my hand in her thin, delicate one, she said, "I was halfway down the road when I remembered I hadn't greeted the minister's wife. I saw in the bulletin that you lived in Guatemala. I lived in Panama years ago."

And then, still holding my hand, she looked me straight in the eye, and in the most undeniably clear Spanish, asked, "*¿Cómo está?*"

Having no idea why I was speechless, Bob prompted, "Talk to her in Spanish."

In a nanosecond, all my plots and plans were sucked out the window in a vortex of oblivion that skipped across the meadow and out of sight. I knew, even though Bob hadn't been officially asked or interviewed, we were moving to Vermont.

But what had really taken my words away, what had left me speechlessly stunned, was the realization that God himself had humored my crazy, improbable, twentieth-century fleece. And by doing so, he had assured me that all would be well.

I stared at the white coiffed curls, the thin, veined hand, the expectant smile, and forced my lips to form a response.

"*Bien*," I said.

I am well.

All is well.

17

A Flatlander and a New England Church

Hope does not disappoint.

The downside of a miracle is the predicament required to precipitate it.

That's also the very place where faith grows. For many of us, that testing ground is in the area of our finances. God's ways often run contrary to man's natural way of thinking. The year I first came to know the Lord, money was scarcer than a ham bone in a Jewish deli. And that's when I read about tithing—giving back at least 10 percent of what I took in.

The Old Testament passage in Malachi says to bring the whole tithe into the storehouse and see if the Lord will not pour out a blessing. I decided to try it. After all, desperate times called for desperate measures. I noted in the back of my Bible: Week 1 income—$45.00; tithe—$5.00.

God is gracious to the simple. The next week I made $145.00. I gave my $15.00 tithe. For the rest of the month, I continued to track my giving and God's provision.

I've since learned he doesn't always respond so readily, but during that time he patiently and personally taught me that I couldn't out-give him. For the following fifteen years or so, I freely gave and abundantly received. So confident was I that I crossed off *finances* on my spiritual growth list as an area I had mastered and would always know, much like driving a car or learning the multiplication table.

But even the DMV retests its senior citizens. And after years of witnessing the faithfulness of heaven, I faced a how-in-the-world-are-we-going-to-live crisis.

The little band of church folk had offered us a salary, which, although it was a generous step of faith for them, amounted to less than we had paid in taxes the previous year. Unlike my quandary in Guatemala, I didn't wonder how I was going to *cook* the food; I wondered how I was going to *afford* it. I knew God was quite able to supply all my needs, but the union paid on Fridays.

Nevertheless, we were just about to accept the position when Bob received an offer to run a job that included a salary and benefit package close to six figures. As much as I would like to think faith only moves forward, I am aware of the propensity to forget past provisions in the face of a new crisis. In an instant I went from faithful to fickle.

"What?" I exclaimed, extending my arm straight out. "On this hand we can have six weeks vacation, medical and dental benefits, a good salary, and retire in a few years with 80 percent pension, or," I said, flapping the other arm, "we can live within spitting distance of the poverty line in a four-room apartment with a salary pledged on faith!"

Although I didn't understand why it seemed the dream thief was succeeding in pocketing my plans, deep within my being—in that spot that has so much substance but can't be touched—I knew in spite of salary or climate or dried-up dreams, we would go. So, in the end, believing faith is indeed "a splendid enterprise," we decided to accept the church's offer and chose to follow after the purpose we believed we were called to, rather than one based on the seeming security of the electrical union. Less than two years after we had packed our possessions for a move south, we again packed them, this time for a journey north.

We moved to Vermont on the tail end of a February blizzard, exactly 174 years after that other bracing February day, in 1822, when two pastors and ten people, believing "it pleased God . . . to visit his people in this place to awaken and reclaim some that were slumbering or wandering, and to convert some to the knowledge of the truth," joined together and formed the Congregational Church at Clarendon (*Clarendon, Vermont: 1761–1976*, Rutland, VT: Academy Books). With the same vision and about as many people, we looked forward to being a part of what God was doing in this little New England town.

The blustery, cold night gave impetus to the air of excitement and adventure as church folk and good-hearted neighbors quickly unloaded our Penske truck and stuffed the contents of our three-bedroom colonial home into the four-room downstairs apartment that served as the parsonage. The upstairs had long ago been sealed off into separate living quarters. With a dwindling church community to maintain it, the two-story clapboard house had fallen into a state of disrepair. A gutter swung from the corner of the eaves. We stepped carefully over the hole in the front porch.

Bob asked one of the men about the severe sag in the kitchen floor, but he assured us that there wasn't a house in Vermont, where, "if you put a marble on one side, it wouldn't roll to the other."

A wreath, still fragrant with the sprigs of cedar, pine, and balsam, hung from the kitchen door, completing the quintessential Vermont country home.

Lily busied herself setting up her room. Gus, the Samoyed we had bought for her when we returned to the States, romped and rolled in the deep snow in an ecstatic celebration of his Arctic ancestry. A few hours later, after many hearty hellos and welcomes, we nodded our thank-yous and good-byes and closed the door of the moving van.

I tunneled around the boxes piled above my head and crawled

into bed. A snowplow rumbled past. I pictured the wave of snow that curled off the wide blade and buried everything beneath its banks as a clean swath was cut in the untraveled road. Uncertain as the outcome was, I had to admit, I liked new beginnings, new paths forged to somewhere. That was the exciting part of traveling with the Lord; you never knew where he might go, but he always made a way. I wanted to embrace his journey, not resign myself to it. The windows rattled as the snowplow thundered past on its return sweep.

Before we had unpacked many boxes, someone in the church died. A few weeks later, someone else died. My father called to advise Bob that he was supposed to be bringing the people in, not putting them six feet under. We were trying to bring them in, but I suspected, eyeing the old organ wedged in the back corner next to the piano and the ancient hymnals, we might lose a few more with some of the changes on the horizon.

Although FOX commentator Bill O'Reilly is convinced Vermont is another country, you still don't need a passport to cross the border. There is, however, a rugged, independent spirit that characterizes the people hewn out of these verdant hills, a spirit the people take great pride in holding. Vermonters don't take kindly to being told what to do; nor do they like change—especially if the change comes from the hands of a flatlander (those rich people from New York or New Jersey who buy up all the land and cause the taxes to go up—a logic that tends to overlook the high taxes those out-of-towners actually pay).

Bob certainly was not rich, but he was a flatlander, a flatlander who was about to learn that though the numbers in our church were few, they were mighty in opinions. We would all go through a lot of hoeing and plowing and voting on the color of pew cushions and hall walls as God once again grew his church in Clarendon.

The heavy door creaked as Bob pulled it open, and we slipped into the darkened sanctuary. We came here at night to pray, to present our longings with all the others that for the past two centuries had been whispered in this place—some in full confidence of heaven's response, some out of Sunday morning ritual, and others in desperate hope that it might be true.

We paused before each pew and could almost see, as though habitual devotion to a certain seat had left their imprint, each person and family cluster. Tradition had strong roots in this place, roots so strong we worried they had squeezed out the remembrance of how very present God is.

Neither Bob nor I had ever stayed in one place long enough to set such deep roots, and as much as we honored tradition, we understood how easily routine dulls the joy of expectation. Bob belted out a song of praise that rose to the high tin ceiling. Suddenly he stopped. We looked at each other as an idea we had previously considered and then shelved out of cowardice burst into being. As we moved to the back corner, where the old piano lingered like a Sunday morning latecomer, we hoped no one in the congregation still believed in settling differences by kicking in the door and demanding justice at the end of a gun barrel. Bob got on one end; I guided the other.

Slowly we rolled the piano out from its place of exile and up the narrow aisle to the front corner right beside the altar.

Perhaps there is no single issue that drives saints to sin faster than a change in the worship part of a service. The music is too loud, too redundant, too modern, and too traditional. Opinions are many, strong, and deeply entrenched. And although our hymnals looked as if they had arrived on the *Mayflower*, and our congregation was as steeped in tradition as a Tetley tea bag in hot water, I will be forever grateful to them for not running us out of church that Sunday morning they found the piano in place of a front pew.

Having survived the move of worship to a front and visible position, Bob gained confidence. So when he heard about a visiting band of young people whose integrity was vouched for by a local pastor, he invited them to play at our church. The group set up their equipment, running more electrical cords than we had outlets for. I was quite sure a set of drums had never before passed the doors of this ancient brick building.

People came; people went. For the most part, however, we were settling in well with these good-hearted, generous people who loved to laugh, and be involved with their kids, and eat pot-luck dinners, and go for rides after a snowstorm just to see if they could make it through before the plow. Most had never heard anyone preach about the supposed evils of baseball games or makeup, or about the differences between Calvinists and Armenians, as is so common in other regions of the country.

By now Bob had his bachelor's degree in theology and was working on his master's in ministry, but he continued to have some of the same difficulties in communication that he had in Guatemala. There is a certain *Christianese* that was spoken in many of our previous church circles, expressions that we took for granted were understood in all church circles.

One Sunday, after the collection had been taken and brought to the front, Bob asked Ben, one of the ushers, if he would "lift up the offering." Bob closed his eyes and waited for the ensuing prayer. Sitting in the front pew, I could see immediately that Ben didn't have a clue what Bob meant, and so he did the most logical thing—he lifted the plate of bills high over his head and waited to see what Bob was going to do. I sat in my seat, willing Bob to open his eyes and relieve the bewildered man.

On another Sunday, Bob caused some raised eyebrows when he announced a video program he was excited about. Someone had donated a series on marriage called *Hidden Keys to Loving Relationships.* Since money was tight for extracurricular materials, Bob was particularly pleased to offer this resource to the congregation, but his tongue ran faster than his mind as he stood at the pulpit and proudly announced that over the next several weeks we would learn how to have *Loving Keys to Hidden Relationships.*

The people appreciated his good-natured transparency and even rewarded him for it. One of the small groups we held in our home focused on the topic of marriage. Hoping to stimulate open discussion and encourage people to be real with one another, Bob used his own marriage as an example in his closing prayer request. Couples bowed their heads as Bob presented his request for his own relationship, "Lord, I ask you for more passion in our marriage."

Not sharing his willingness to bare our lives in public places, I squinted my eyes to keep them from popping wide open, but peered through a slit under my lashes across the circle to where he was so fervently praying.

"You want passion?" I muttered to myself. "Don't worry. As soon as everyone is out the door, you are going to see some passion," I promised.

As news does, it got around. That year, thanks to a friend who had connections with a local country inn, the church gave us a complimentary weekend suite complete with in-room Jacuzzi.

In time, baptisms, baby dedications, and weddings began outnumbering burials. The Lord had even answered Bob's prayer for more contemporary hymnals. Shortly after the finance committee had adamantly turned down Bob's request, saying there was no new hymnal money, a woman approached Bob and told him the company she worked for was willing to donate their returned items if we wanted to have a yard sale. Yard sales rated right up alongside Sunday drives and strawberry festivals, so we cleaned the piles of useless things that had collected in the belfry and the hall and set out tables. At the end of the day, Bob counted up the bills and box of change. It came to the exact amount we needed to place new hymnals in every pew.

Meanwhile, Mrs. Howard, the woman who had hand-delivered my Spanish-speaking answer from the Lord, and I met each week to play chess and practice Spanish, which was all that remained, or so I thought, from my mission days in Central America.

Although I was excited about what God was doing on the church front, I harbored two personal disappointments—one that I didn't have my own home and could see no way that we would ever be able to afford one; the other that our experience in Guatemala was growing fainter. My private life was pockmarked with a lot of whining and grousing. Reflecting on the biblical admonition that any works not built on Christ would be burned, I imagined the glow filling the eastern horizon of heaven as my works went up in a bonfire if I didn't stop throwing myself pity parties.

The Vermont landscape is one of nature's showoffs, especially in the fall, when, with a sweeping flourish, the hillsides explode in a grand finale of crimsons, purples, golds, and russets—dazzling reminders during the cold, dark days to come that to everything there is a season. Before our first season in this Northern outpost drew to a close, the Lord showed me there was nothing I had given up that he couldn't give back, pressed down and flowing over, even if what I really deserved from all my grousing was a lickin'.

The mailman pulled up to the house, which would have been an otherwise unremarkable occurrence except for the fact that he got out and came to the door. I watched curiously as he stepped up to the porch. My mind rapidly inventoried the possibilities of mail important enough to be hand delivered. I was pretty sure I hadn't entered any sweepstakes within the past six months; neither did I have a stash of delinquent parking tickets in my glove compartment. As I signed for the fat envelope, I noted the return address for a law firm. I removed the thick sheets.

We had heard of the sudden death of one of our relatives, but what we had not known was that she had some money and had named us among her heirs. In a totally unexpected turn of events, just like that—the moment after the impossible—we were able to go out and buy a house.

Although we had never seen anything affordable for sale in our targeted area, we decided to give it one more look. As we slowly circled the block for the hundredth time in the past few months, I imagined the eyes peering behind white lace curtains, on neighborhood alert for our red Toyota pickup.

The For Sale sign appeared out of nowhere, as if the earth had just opened up and birthed a shiny metal shrub. Bob downshifted and pulled into the long driveway. Gravel crunched beneath our tires as we approached the house, sitting on a sun-drenched knoll like a silent doorman awaiting our arrival. We walked around the back. A canopy of overgrown junipers and crab apples sheltered a large, secluded stone patio, reminiscent of Antiguan ruins. Neither of us spoke as we absorbed the surroundings. I had no idea how much the house cost; I had no idea what it even looked like inside, but I knew this was the house—my house.

Less than a year before, I had wondered how we would afford

to live if Bob gave up his lucrative union job to follow God's call to Vermont, and now, there we were, in a dazzling defiance of the rules of self-provision—debt-free with a beautiful home and two cars.

Meanwhile, the postman (who as far as I could tell, didn't glow or bear the name Gabriel), wasn't through being the messenger of life-changing news. Another letter he delivered that fall bore a Guatemalan postmark. Tim and Dena wrote to say they would be in the States and would be able to come to Vermont for a visit.

I fingered the thin onion-skin air mail paper and thought about that day in the village when we saw Tim rumbling by on his three-wheeler towing a wagon full of kids. Now he was going to be our Vermont church's first guest missionary. It seemed like a rather elaborate way to go about getting a speaker. Although I was sure the One who designed this complex universe was well aware that a straight line is the shortest distance between two points, I delighted in the way he chose to ignore the fact. And I began to suspect he wasn't finished with our Guatemala connection after all.

18

South of the Border Again

I used to think everything depended on me. What a relief to know God is in control of my life. His plans and purposes are far more marvelous than ones I could ever conjure up myself.

I stood in front of the congregation and surveyed the expectant faces, uncertain how they would react to my proposal. Old Joe snoozed in the back pew, but he would probably have an opinion anyway. I suspected Rupert would be as obdurate as the wild donkey the neighbors installed in the sheep pen to keep out the coyotes. Phyllis might be persuaded even though she believed we had enough poor people right here without having to go out of the country to find any. Tom and Kathy undoubtedly would be supportive, as would Anita, if the sparkle in her eyes was any indication.

Tim and Dena's visit, while they were in the States on furlough the previous fall, had both sparked our church's interest in missions and kindled the possibility in my mind for expanding our vision. Not only did I want to increase our financial support to missions, I wanted to take a team on a short-term trip to Mexico.

Knowing my interest, my brother Bill, a pastor in Maine, invited us to join his church's annual mission trip. We would be working with a Christian medical outreach, Mexican Medical, in Cabo San Lucas on the tip of the Baja.

I didn't know how many of the handful of people staring back at me had crossed any international borders lately, but I suspected not many. Taking courage from the small numbers and the unusual circumstances that birthed the American Mission Movement, I recounted the story of the five men who in 1808 first prayed about organizing foreign missions while taking shelter in a New England haystack during a thunderstorm.

Don't despise the day of small beginnings, I thought, looking over the pews.

After the service, three men approached me: Tom, a carpenter; Ernie, a man who had traveled the Vermont back roads most of his life; and Ira, a ponytailed man as short on words as on displays of emotions. They'd be interested in going, they said. And with about as much fanfare as an afternoon rock in the old porch chair, the Brick Church at Clarendon formed its first mission team. Bob, Lily, and I dug out our passports.

Our flight was late. We needed to hurry to make the next connection, but the security scanner was adamant. The man in front of us had to take off his prosthetic leg so they could check it for contraband. He calmly offered it for inspection, then hailed a ride on one of the club carts that managed to whiz through the crowds of luggage-toting passengers without knocking any of them off their feet. We raced alongside. The flight attendant urged us to hurry to our seats. Within minutes of locking our seat belts, the huge craft raced down the runway, carrying our empty supply trunks, souvenir-filled bags, and overflowing hearts homeward.

Tom looked across the aisle and gave me a thumbs-up and satisfied nod before closing his eyes and giving in to exhaustion. I was sure I could see the presleep images panning across his mind: the cardboard-and-tin-house villages, the throngs of excited children running to greet our bus and receive their hugs and stories and gifts from the gringos, the stoic mothers carrying sick children to be examined by the medical team in the makeshift space in the back of the bus or to be examined themselves for long-suffered illness probably requiring more than the aspirin or antibiotics we would have—the pleading eyes, grasping for the imparted hope of our prayers and presence that transcended language barriers.

Some contend that short-term mission trips are glorified feel-good vacations at the expense of money that could better be used for long-term projects. But as I watched the faces of our first team, I knew they were each going to take back a report that would excite others and ignite a committed involvement that would travel far beyond the confines of our pews.

One by one overhead lights dimmed as the aircraft forged its way north through the dark night. It had certainly been a fulfilling week, made possible by the generosity of our little "flock," and I hadn't even seen it coming. In my grand moment of self-sacrifice, I thought I had laid down my dream, but God had picked it up and handed it back to me—perhaps he would do it again. I stared out my porthole-shaped window at the blinking wing light and thought, *Hmm, maybe next year we could go to . . .*

In one of those divine coincidences, as we were preparing for our third mission trip to the Baja, we received news that Pat and Graci, the couple who had helped us greatly in Guatemala, had moved to La Paz, Mexico, a few hours up the eastern coast from where the Mexican Medical base was located. Their house had lots of space to board a team, and their yard could easily host a medical/VBS outreach. A few weeks later, once again teamed up with Mex Med, we arrived on their doorstep with our Vermont team.

Pat stirred the pot of black beans and rice; the smell of garlicky plantain followed me up the stairs as I showed our team where to put their sleeping bags. Out in the yard, other team members assembled the nine-foot-tall Goliath we would use for a skit.

Excited kids poked each other with animal balloons and settled down on the spread-out tarps.

As dusk fell, Rachel, a member of our team blessed with one of those alto voices that rises from a back-row pew and floats over the sanctuary with the impact of a celestial choir, stepped up to the portable microphone. One hundred squirming children stilled as she began singing "Shout to the Lord" in perfect Spanish. The long queue of people waiting patiently to see the doctor turned their heads in unison as the rich, full notes of her voice rose above the settling dusk and drifted through the barrio. "All of my days, I will sing praise to the wonders of your mighty love."

The wind that had scattered us from Guatemala to Vermont, and Pat and Graci to Mexico, had also blown through the lives of Tim and Dena. The year after we left the village, Tim and Dena turned the daily administration of their well-organized children's home and feeding centers over to another couple and moved to Costa Rica, where they established another home for abused children. Although they spent most of their time in Costa Rica, they still returned to Guatemala for several weeks out of the year to oversee visiting mission teams, lend their wise support to the leaders, and dish out lots of hugs to their beloved orphans.

We kept in touch after they had visited us in Vermont, and after three trips to Cabo with Mexican Medical, we shifted our attention to their children's home in Costa Rica. As team leader, I felt a great responsibility for the safety of the people with me, but I didn't worry as much about taking a team to Costa Rica as I did whenever I contemplated taking one back to Guatemala.

Visitors were both welcomed and warned immediately upon arrival at the airport in San José, Costa Rica. Huge murals advertising fun things to do, like zip-lining through the rain forests, were suspended next to prominent signs issuing stern warnings to anyone caught harming the country's children. This was a place where we could drink the water, ride roads free of bandits, and hope for the strong arm of the law if needed.

We piled into the van; Tim hoisted himself behind the wheel. About ten minutes down the road, one of my teammates turned to me, her eyes round in realization. "Wait a minute," she whispered. "Isn't he paralyzed from the waist down?"

Tim did a little jerky thing with the wheel and muttered something about the brakes.

"Yes, he is," I said. Knowing that one of the first fears everyone has to overcome in another country involves traveling on the breathtaking roads, I decided not to say anything about the hand controls his car was equipped with.

Little children shouted, "Tim, Tim," and ran up to the car as we pulled through the iron gates. A young boy, high up in the lofty branches of a mango tree, tossed his plump pickings to the ground and scurried down.

The various buildings in the sprawling compound were linked by sidewalks, which made getting around easier for the children with handicaps, as well as for Tim in his wheelchair. Although I never heard him complain, I knew the rocky roads and dirt paths in the village in Guatamala were difficult to maneuver.

We unloaded our bags and went off to hold babies, kick balls, and get our job lists. Knowing Tim, it would be ambitious. He had probably designed more buildings and drawn up more projects from the seat of his wheeled world than many an architect in a Manhattan high-rise. Dena had arranged for us to do some presentations at the school. I was content to come alongside these faithful people and do whatever they needed or wanted, be it physical, emotional, or spiritual support.

It was still dark when I woke. Assorted snorts, wheezes, and whistling sounds played in discordant harmony as the other team members slept deep under their blankets. No one dared expose any more skin than they had to for fear that a night creature would crawl across them. I slid down from the top bunk and tried not to step on Kathy below me, but she woke. We slipped on our flip-flops, put on a pot of coffee, and tiptoed out to the porch.

Kathy searched among the constellations for the one that told the greatest story—the Southern Cross. We caught a glimpse of it sliding into the horizon behind Tim and Dena's house.

At our feet, millions of leaf cutter ants, each holding upright a wedge of leaf like a tiny green umbrella, filed by in precise formation along the edge of the patio and disappeared into an opening in the ground. Other than our lone witness, the only evidence of this nocturnal marvel would be a newly naked tree in the morning. From the majestic to the miniscule, I longed to absorb the beauty in my being. Just then a dark shape flickered by the inside light.

"A bat is in the house," Kathy said calmly, slowly opening the door. Being a forester, she was more comfortable with wildlife than I was. I grabbed the camcorder and followed her as she tracked the flitting shadow to an empty room. The rest of the team slept, unaware that fearless Kathy was protecting them from a rude awakening.

After she chased the bat out, we settled back in our porch chairs to watch the sunrise, listen for the long-tailed motmot's morning song, and plan how we would surprise the others with the video of all the goings-on we protected them from while they were sleeping.

Every afternoon, after siesta, we watched the kids work the soccer ball up and down the field in front of our house. Bob thought he needed to stir up some excitement and boasted that five grown gringos could whup a whole team of the Costa Rican fancy-footers in a game any day. The next morning someone hung a crayoned notice on the school wall: *Fútbol competencia a 4:00—Gringos contra Ticos* (as Costa Ricans like to call themselves).

Dena and I sat together on the grass and watched along with the handful of housemothers, who blew bottles of bubbles for the younger children and herded the toddlers off the field. Everyone whooped and hollered as Gabriela, the six-year-old goalie for the Ticos, intercepted Bob's kick on goal. The Ticos raced back down the field and scored. So much for Bob's dare. The feisty kids, with an average age of ten, beat the adult gringos 5-2.

"I love it here," Dena said as she gathered up her things, "but my heart is really in Guatemala."

"A part of mine still is too," I admitted with a resigned sigh.

"Why don't you take a team to the village next year?" Dena asked. "We'll meet you there."

I relished the possibility of finally taking a team from our Vermont church back to our Mayan village so many years after we had uttered those tinny promises of returning. I had been reluctant to return with a team for the same reason I had been hesitant about going the first time—fear for someone else's well-being. But by now many of our church members were strong in their faith. They could decide whether to trust God with their own lives, as could I.

19

A Drunk and a Dream Fulfilled

Nothing, absolutely nothing, is impossible with God.

The donkey ran up to the rickety post-and-wire fence and brayed jubilantly as we got out of the car. He had come to expect a little handout of crackers or bagels or whatever Bob was munching on when he arrived at the church office every morning. Bob had been slipping him some of the doughnuts that Phyllis made for the social hour after Sunday service, but when the head of hospitality got wind of what the pastor was doing with her doughnuts, she put her foot down.

For the past several years, Bob had been the pastor of this little Vermont-town church, which unexpectedly became part of the answer to the question that had so haunted me after returning from Guatemala: What was that all about? A rural New England church hardly seemed the place to find out. But then, that is one of the marvelous things about God—he can do anything, any way he chooses.

I collected the trunks filled with crafts, gifts, and supplies for the orphanage in Guatemala that the team had finished packing the day before. Bob peered at the scale as I stood on it with one of the trunks—two pounds to spare. We were ready to go.

We had dropped them off at a cow pasture airstrip in Guatemala, met them at glistening airport in Costa Rica, and now were searching the crowd for their faces outside the railed barriers of the airport in Guatemala City. Our porters followed Dena as she waved them toward the trucks, where they piled our trunks and bags. The team split up into separate vehicles. I was so excited, I didn't even blink when Dena casually mentioned the truck she was driving stalled out when she applied the brakes. So what if someone would have to jump out and put a stone behind the tire until she got it going. We'd simply add our rocks to the many others that littered the road.

"I was able to get word to Mita and the twins that you were coming," she said, "but I couldn't find Marco."

A barb of disappointment snagged my joy. We had looked forward to seeing our dear little sidekick, who I guessed was in his early twenties by now. I had brought him some gifts, including a picture of Lily, his *gringita* friend, herself now a lovely nineteen-year-old woman. But the thrill of being back in Guatemala and being able to share our village with our Vermont church soon overrode the sadness I felt at this news.

Modernity had found its way into the highlands. Bridges formed pathways over rivers we had once driven through. Dena told us the village even had a few telephones. Our little caravan arrived in town in late afternoon. The pervasive cloud of dust, like a gatekeeper to the village, followed us to the beginning of the cobblestone street, then floated to the ground.

Maybe there were telephones and computers with Internet access prominently displayed on doily-covered tables behind some of the adobe walls, but to all outward appearance, with the exception of young men with iPod earbud wires dangling beneath their straw hats, little had changed. Dogs and pigs and chickens scattered in front of our truck. Dark-haired women in traditional orange-striped skirts with armfuls of babies or baskets stood in doorways. I looked closely at the faces as we passed. The elderly señora from whom we had often bought the sweet breads she baked in her earthen ovens, still stood in her doorway as though the shadow of time had passed her by.

Although more compact than the sprawling children's home in Costa Rica, the children's home in Guatemala reflected that same order, joy, and sense of well-being. A row of babies sat in high chairs and played with their food. Sounds of laughter accompanied the *pat-pat* of hands as young women shaped the day's tortillas in the kitchen. Anita, one of our team members, scooped up a curly-haired toddler and followed Tim as he wheeled over the rocky yard, pointing out our projects.

After getting settled in our respective male/female bunk rooms, we gathered around a bonfire for a cookout in honor of the visiting teams. As happy as if they were all on holiday, children and staff alike ate hot dogs, poked at the glowing embers, and in turn, gave thanks for all they had.

It was pitch-black. I sat up in my top bunk as far as I could without touching the ceiling. I was sure someone had called my name, but all the other women appeared to be asleep.

"Marcia."

"What?" I whispered to the disembodied voice.

"Marcia," it called again more urgently.

Again, I answered "What?" A small beam of light flickered on the far wall. For a moment I flashed back to the scene thousands of years ago when God called the young boy Samuel three times during the night. Perhaps God was giving me a midnight summons, but I wasn't recognizing his voice. I sat up straighter. A noise outside the window caught my attention. My heavenly caller, clad in flimsy pajamas, waved her flashlight. Apparently, Dolores had made a bathroom run and locked herself out of our room.

Giggling, I slid off my bunk and let her in. Later, as I lay there, I wondered if the other women in the room would have had the same expectation I did that God was calling them. Belief in the reality of God's presence was central to my Christian health. Like checking the night sky in hopes of catching that precise moment a shooting star blazed by, I watched for "evidence of things unseen" in my daily life. *Not getting a commission call tonight,* I thought, unaware of the special gift heading my way.

Dena knew we desired to share the gospel in the community, as well as work at the children's home, and had made arrangements for us to visit a remote hillside school where no teams had ever gone. We piled into the back of two rattling pickups, gasped and uttered phrases like "Oh my" as we drove through a wide and briskly moving river, and braced ourselves to jump as we chugged up muddy slopes. The indomitable trucks delivered us safely to our destination at the base of a grassy hill.

We lugged our trunks of supplies up a trail to a long adobe building perched on the edge of the hillside. The front school-yard—all twenty feet wide—ended abruptly at the edge of the steep drop-off. Villagers as well as schoolchildren had gathered under the overhang of the concrete porch. A wrinkled old woman stopped stirring her pot of boiling liquid refreshment and greeted me with a hug. I didn't know why she singled me out, but I felt cloaked in honor.

The team lined up and faced the school group, who had no idea what to expect. Although many of the children spoke their native language, they understood enough Spanish to realize we were singing some silly interactive songs. After a round or two, old, wizened women waved their arms and stomped their feet along with the schoolchildren. Even the suave teenage boys leaning against the wall shed their machismo and attempted to follow some of the rapid movements as we all leaped across cultural chasms.

After settling everyone down, we slowly unrolled an eighteen-foot painted canvas mural that illustrated the days of creation. Quiet, as absolute as the falling sunshine, settled over the group as they heard for the first time the ancient story of the God who created them and the God who loved them. I looked at the engrossed, saucer-eyed faces and breathed a silent prayer of thanks for being witness to this "first" in someone's life, for the privilege of bearing words of life.

Later in the week, as we were gathered at the picnic tables for lunch, someone knocked at the gate. There, framed in the open doorway, like a snapshot in heaven's photo album, waiting shyly for permission to enter, stood our dear friends Mita and her daughter, Julia. I gathered some lunch plates and ushered them to an empty table.

This unusual reunion caught the attention of Anna, Dena's very bright and inquisitive eight-year-old Costa Rican daughter. She slid onto the edge of my chair and listened as I asked Mita and Julia about their lives. Mita had left the project and moved back to her mountain village. Both of her daughters had married. Blanca was working in Guatemala City, a big journey for a girl who had never been outside her village, but I couldn't understand what Julia was trying to tell me about her own husband.

Little Anna, wise beyond her years, summed it up for me. "He's bad," she said. Julia shrugged and gave me a resigned smile as if to say, "That's the way it is."

After lunch, Mita gathered her plastic shopping bag and prepared to leave. We shared a bittersweet hug that I suspected would be our last. It had been so good to see them. I wished we could have seen Marco too.

I woke up on the morning of our last day in the village as sick as the proverbial dog. Everyone on the team had dutifully minded my admonition not to drink anything but bottled beverages, but I, in an irrational moment of camaraderie, had drunk some of the mush the old Mayan woman at the school had offered from her boiling pot. Dreading a four-hour ride on a gussied-up school bus with no bathroom, I dragged myself from my bed and tossed down some Imodium. The bus Dena hired to take us to Panajachel honked at the gate. Apparently the other team members had already packed the trunks and piled them in the yard for the *ayudante* to secure on top.

Bob stepped into the bunk room. I thought he looked exceptionally happy for a man whose wife was in the throes of death. Unable to contain himself, he blurted, "Marsh, the bus is here, and guess who the *ayudante* is!" From the joy that bounced off his face, I knew he was referring to a young, barefoot, lazy-eyed, bus-chasing street waif. Words spoken years before echoed in my mind—"Marco, you're the best. You should be an *ayudante* someday."

Dena stood beside me as we watched Marco scamper across the top of the bus to retrieve the trunk containing his gifts. "You know what's really amazing," she said, wrapping her arms around my very sick shoulders, "Marco isn't the regular *ayudante* for this bus company. He wasn't supposed to be here this morning."

Apparently wanting to put his signature touch on his surprise, God had arranged that when the regularly scheduled *ayudante* got drunk the night before and couldn't work, the bus company would borrow Marco from another bus—just for us—just because he loves us.

Dolores whipped her head around and rolled her wide eyes at me as the bus raced around the switchback, narrowly missing the oncoming truck packed with people. I was too sick to care. We all slid across the worn, vinyl seats as the bus careened around yet another curve. Dena quietly approached the driver and told him to slow down. I clutched the sick bag I had kept from the plane and fixed my eyes on the young man standing in the front of the bus. I noted his new work boots, clean jeans, and shirt. He kept glancing down at the photo of a young woman that he had propped on the dash.

"Marco looks so good, Lord. You saved the best for last. I love your surprises. Thank you."

As I looked around the bus, I thought of all the people we had been able to take to the mission field because of connections we made that year we had so blindly followed God to a remote village on a Mayan mountainside.

Then, the move to the church in Vermont had seemed so random—so disconnected from anything we were planning, and yet it all fit together. From Guatemala to Vermont to Mexico, Costa Rica, and finally back again to Guatemala. At each leg of the journey, I saw the handiwork of the One who makes cowards courageous, ordinary lives purposeful, and dried-up dreams fruitful.

The dream thief slunk away empty-handed. My heart overflowed with the goodness of the Lord. His ways were not my ways, they were better. They were perfect. We had come full circle.

Epilogue: Five Years Later

During the night a heavy snowfall draped the yard in a thick, white shroud. Appreciating both the beauty and the snow day from school, I poured a cup of coffee and watched the morning sun set off a myriad of colorful prisms as it played across the icy crystals.

We had been in Vermont for eleven years. Bob loved the part he had played in growing a church. I totally enjoyed my role as an English/lit teacher at the Rutland Area Christian School, and I especially appreciated the opportunity to lead seven mission teams to three different countries in Latin America. We had grown close to our Vermont family of friends, but a certainty that our sojourn in Vermont was over, that we had done what we had come to do, jarred our peace. As convinced as we were that our time had ended here, we were unsure about what to do or where to go next. One thing we knew—the God who had directed our steps this far was still in control.

I looked out my window at the expanse of unbroken snow and considered my options—to sit and admire its pristine beauty or to go make tracks.

Pulling on my boots and mittens, I stepped out into the dazzling daylight.